The Real World of Democracy

by
C. B. Macpherson

Oxford University Press
New York and Oxford

First issued by the Canadian Broadcasting Corporation, 1965

First published by the Clarendon Press, 1966

First issued at Oxford University Press, New York,
1972

printing, last digit: 20 19 18 17

Preface

What is here presented is the text of the Massey Lectures first broadcast by the Canadian Broadcasting Corporation in January and February, 1965. In preparing lectures for both radio broadcast and printed publication, one must decide whether to sacrifice the listener to the reader, or the reader to the listener. Those who heard the lectures discerned that the listener had been sacrificed. The reader, wishing that parts of the argument had been more fully presented, may find that there is still too much compression. Such compression was unavoidable in treating this subject in six half-hour lectures. To have rewritten and extended them would have meant a long delay in publication, and a final text which would probably have satisfied neither the specialist nor the general reader to whom the lectures are addressed. They are therefore presented here as they were originally prepared: a few passages omitted from the spoken lectures to keep them within the limits of broadcast time, are now restored.

University of Toronto   C. B. Macpherson

Contents

**The Real World
of Democracy**

————————————————————

1   Old and New Dimensions of Democracy

There is a good deal of muddle about democracy. I mean not that democracy itself consists of muddling through (though this could be argued), but that our thinking about democracy is muddled. This is partly due to boredom. We are tired of hearing that democracy is in crisis, tired of being asked anxiously to furbish up the image of democracy. We would rather get on with the business of living. So we don't give it much of a thought. Or if we do, we are apt to be put off by the confusion we find in what we read and hear about it. At bottom, the muddle about democracy is due to a genuine confusion as to what democracy is supposed to be about. For the word democracy has changed its meaning more than once, and in more than one direction.

Democracy used to be a bad word. Everybody who was anybody knew that democracy, in its original sense of rule by the people or government in accordance with the will of the bulk of the people, would be a bad thing — fatal to individual freedom and to all the graces of civilized living. That was the position taken by pretty nearly all men of intelligence from the earliest historical times down to about a hundred years ago. Then, within fifty years, democracy became a good thing. Its full acceptance into the ranks of respectability was apparent by the time of the

First World War, a war which the Western allied leaders could proclaim was fought to make the world safe for democracy. Since then, in the last fifty years, democracy has remained a good thing — so much so that everybody claims to have it. Revolutions have been made against our kind of democracy — our Western liberal democracy — in the name of proletarian democracy, of 'people's democracy' and of several varieties of African and Asian democracy. And these revolutions have altered the face of the world quite considerably. Democracy has become an ambiguous thing, with different meanings — even apparently opposite meanings — for different peoples.

It is clear that the real world of democracy has changed. And it is probable that it will go on changing. We in the West are gradually realizing that the West no longer has a monopoly of civilization or world leadership. Old habits of thought die hard. It has not been easy to give up the assumption that the future was bound to go our way. It was a fair enough assumption until a few decades ago. Most of the backward countries were in colonial tutelage to liberal-democratic states, and it was assumed that before being granted independence they were to be brought along to the point where they would run themselves on liberal-democratic lines. True, one substantial part of the world had rejected the liberal-democratic way as early as 1917, with the Russian revolution and the formation of the Soviet Union. But until the Second World War, this could be regarded in the West as something outside the mainstream of world development, and even as something bound to break down and revert ultimately to the otherwise dominant pattern.

In the last twenty years all this has changed. The Soviet Union is no longer considered unviable: its achievements during the war and its subsequent technological advances have made this clear. Most of Eastern Europe has been brought into the Soviet orbit, and is no longer regarded as likely to move into the liberal-democratic pattern. China has moved entirely outside the Western orbit. And on top of all this, most of the underdeveloped areas of Africa and South and East Asia have achieved independence in circumstances which have led them to become one-party states. With few exceptions they have not moved into the Soviet camp (nor do I think they are likely to do so) but they have pretty decisively rejected both the ethos and the actual institutions of our individualist liberal-democracy. And all these countries consider themselves to be democracies.

So the dimensions of democracy have changed in this one quite obvious way. Liberal-democratic. nations can no longer expect to run the world, nor can they expect that the world will run to them. It is not easy to get used to this idea, but we are getting used to it, and, perforce, our governments are adjusting themselves to the new facts. Nevertheless, we in the West have built up a system which we value very highly. It combines a large measure of individual liberty with a fair approximation to majority rule. None of the other systems have managed this, and we don't intend to be talked out of our achievement no matter how necessary a policy of co-existence with the other systems may be.

The question I want to raise is whether we are likely to lose our unique system by our own doing, or on what terms can we keep it? It is no use digging our heels in unless we can be sure we are on solid ground. How much is the ground of democracy shifting? How far, if at all, must we change, and in what directions, if our system is to continue to serve the purposes we want it to serve, and is to continue to embody the values of freedom and individuality that we have always meant it to embody? And what are the prospects of the other systems—the non-liberal democracies—changing in ways that would bring them closer to us? And finally, how far do the two kinds of change depend on each other: does the possibility of the others changing, in a direction that we would like, depend on the way we change? Can we keep what is really valuable in our democracy while adjusting ourselves sufficiently to the new world to acknowledge their claims to co-existence with us?

These are some of the questions that need to be looked at. To look at them clearly we need to pay attention to certain facts which are easily, and often, overlooked. One such fact, to which I have already referred, is that democracy is not properly to be equated with our unique Western liberal-democracy, but that the clearly non-liberal systems which prevail in the Soviet countries, and the somewhat different non-liberal systems of most of the underdeveloped countries of Asia and Africa, have a genuine historical claim to the title democracy. I shall come back to this fact, and some of its implications, in the second lecture, and later on as well.

A second fact is that our liberal-democracy, like any other system, is a system of power; that it is, indeed, again like any other, a double system of power. It is a system by which people can be *governed*, that is, made to do things they would not otherwise do, and made to refrain from doing things they otherwise might do. Democracy as a system of government is, then, a system by which power is exerted by the state over individuals and groups within it. But more than that, a democratic government, like any other, exists to uphold and enforce a certain kind of society, a certain set of relations between individuals, a certain set of rights and claims that people have on each other both directly, and indirectly through their rights to property. These relations themselves are relations of power—they give different people, in different capacities, power over others.

A third fact, which some people find admirable and some people would prefer not to have mentioned, is that liberal-democracy and capitalism go together. Liberal-democracy is found only in countries whose economic system is wholly or predominantly that of capitalist enterprise. And, with few and mostly temporary exceptions, every capitalist country has a liberal-democratic political system. It would be surprising if this close correspondence between liberal-democracy and capitalism were merely co-incidental, and I shall spend some time in later lectures examining this relation.

When we have grasped such facts as the three just mentioned, and have explored their implications, we should be able to reduce in some measure the current uncertainties about democracy, and to see a little more clearly where we are going and where we might go.

Let us begin by looking at the old and the new dimensions of democracy. I said at the beginning that until about a hundred years ago democracy was a bad thing, that in the next fifty years it became a good thing, and that in the last fifty years it has become an ambiguous thing. I have said also that the current non-liberal systems have some historical title to call themselves democracies. What has happened? Two changes have taken place in the concept of democracy, one change in our Western societies, and one in the Soviet and the underdeveloped worlds.

In our Western societies the democratic franchise was not installed until after the liberal society and the liberal state were firmly established. Democracy came as a top dressing. It had to accommodate itself to the soil that had already been prepared by the operation of the competitive, individualist, market society, and by the operation of the liberal state, which served that society through a system of freely competing though not democratic political parties. It was the liberal state that was democratized, and in the process, democracy was liberalized. That is one change in the nature of democracy, which we shall explore further in a moment.

In the rest of the world—in the present Soviet countries and the now newly-independent underdeveloped countries—democracy, we may say, came as a revolution against the liberal capitalist society and state. The political movements that came to power there thought of themselves, and do now think of themselves, as democratic. For them democracy has had something like its original meaning, government by or for the common people, by or for the hitherto oppressed classes. Yet here too the meaning has changed, though not in the same direction as in the liberal world. By the time democratic movements became strong in the economically unadvanced countries, the productivity of modern machine technology had so increased and was so increasing that it had become possible to think of a future of plenty for all. Hence in these countries they could, and did, and do, think of democracy not in its original meaning as rule in the interests of a class, but as rule in the interests of the whole people, transcending classes.

This change in the notion of democracy in the non-Western world is less familiar and more complex than the change in the Western world, but both changes will repay some attention. I shall use the rest of this lecture to look a little more closely into the change in the idea of democracy in the Western world, reserving the other change for the next two lectures.

Democracy originally meant rule by the common people, the plebeians. It was very much a class affair: it meant the sway of the lowest and largest class. That is why it was feared and rejected by men of learning, men of substance, men who valued civilized ways of life. Democracy, as a levelling doctrine, was rejected by Plato in the fifth century B.C., and no less explicitly by Cromwell in the seventeenth century A.D. It was even rejected by Cromwell's left-wing allies in the English civil war, the so-called Levellers, who split from him on the issue of who should have the vote. Even they did not think of extending the vote to the two-thirds of the nation who were either wage-earners, or recipients of poor relief, or both. Such men, they held, were dependent on others, and so not entitled to a political voice. Even the chief nineteenth-century apostle of liberalism, John Stuart Mill, who realized that the common people had now to be treated as people, proposed a system of voting that would prevent the labouring class having a majority voice.

The claims of democracy would never have been admitted in the present liberal-democracies had those countries not got a solid basis of liberalism first. The liberal democracies that we know were liberal first and democratic later. To put this in another way, before democracy came in the Western world there came the society and the politics of choice, the society and politics of competition, the society and politics of the market. This was the liberal society and state. It will be obvious that I am using liberal here in a very broad sense. I use it in what I take to be its essential sense, to mean that both the society as a whole and the system of government were organized on a principle of freedom of choice.

In society as a whole, that is, in all those relations between individuals other than the political relation of governors and governed, the principle of free choice was acknowledged. The principle was even insisted upon—for it was sometimes truer in theory than in practice. Individuals were free to choose their religion, their pattern of life, their marriage partners, their occupations. They were free to make the best arrangements, the best bargain they could, in everything that affected their living. They offered their services, their products, their savings, or their labour, on the market and got the market price, which was itself determined by all their independent decisions. With the income they got they made more choices—how much to spend, how much to save, what to spend on, and what to invest in. They made these decisions in the light of the going prices, and their decisions in turn made the prices, and so determined what would be produced, that is, determined how the whole energies and accumulated capital of the society would be allotted between different possible uses.

This was the market economy. In its fully developed form, when most individuals offered their labour on the market to those who possessed accumulated capital on which they could employ other people's labour, it is known as the capitalist market economy. When it was established—and it was established in the now advanced countries between the seventeenth and the nineteenth centuries—it was an enormously liberalizing force. It changed not just the economic arrangements but the whole society. Instead of a society based on custom, on status, and on authoritarian allocation of work and rewards, you had a society based on individual mobility, on contract, and on impersonal market allocation of work and rewards in response to individual choices. Everyone was swept into the free market, and all his relations with others were increasingly converted to market relations.

Previously, people had been, and had thought of themselves as, not individuals but members of ranks or orders or communities. Their fairly fixed place in a customary society had given them some security but little freedom. Now, people began, with delight or with fear, to think of themselves as individuals free to choose. Indeed they were compelled to be free. Students of political philosophy will be familiar with Jean-Jacques Rousseau's paradox that in the good society men would be forced to be free. The fact is that before he wrote men were already being forced to be free. Rousseau's compulsive freedom was offered as an antidote to the compulsive freedom that had already set in in fact.

This society based on individual choices had of course some drawbacks. There was, necessarily, great inequality, for you cannot have a capitalist market society unless some people have got accumulated capital and a great many others have none, or have so little that they cannot work on their own but have to offer their labour to others. This involves inequality in freedom of choice: all are free but some are freer than others. Nevertheless, the productivity of the capitalist system was greatly superior to that of any previous system, and there was more chance of moving up (as well as down), and besides there had always been inequality, so the new freedom was held to be a net gain. In any case the new system took root and produced the liberal individualist society. There was nothing democratic about it, in any sense of equality of real right, but it was liberal.

To make this society work, or to allow it to operate, a non-arbitrary, or responsible, system of government was needed. And this was provided, by revolutionary action in England in the seventeenth century, in America in the eighteenth, in France in the eighteenth and nineteenth, and by a variety of methods in most other Western countries sometime within those centuries. What was established was a system whereby the government was put in a sort of market situation. The government was treated as the supplier of certain political goods—not just the political good of law and order in general, but the specific political goods demanded by those who had the upper hand in running that particular kind of society. What was needed was the kind of laws and regulations, and tax structure, that would make the market society work, or allow it to work, and the kind of state services—defence, and even military expansion, education, sanitation, and various sorts of assistance to industry, such as tariffs and grants for railway development—that were thought necessary to make the system run efficiently and profitably. These were the kinds of political goods that were wanted. But how was the demand to call forth the supply? How to make government responsive to the choices of those it was expected to cater to? The way was of course to put governmental power into the hands of men who were made subject to periodic elections at which there was a choice of candidates and parties. The electorate did not need to be a democratic one, and as a general rule was not; all that was needed was an electorate consisting of the men of substance, so that the government would be responsive to their choices.

To make this political choice an effective one, there had to be certain other liberties. There had to be freedom of association—that is, freedom to form political parties, and freedom to form the kind of associations we now know as pressure groups, whose purpose is to bring to bear on parties and on governments the combined pressure of the interests they represent. And there had to be freedom of speech and publication, for without these the freedom of association is of no use. These freedoms could not very well be limited to men of the directing classes. They had to be demanded in principle for everybody. The risk that the others would use them to get a political voice was a risk that had to be taken.

So came what I am calling the liberal state. Its essence was the system of alternate or multiple parties whereby governments could be held responsible to different sections of the class or classes that had a political voice. There was nothing necessarily democratic about the responsible party system. In the country of its origin, England, it was well established, and working well, half a century or a century before the franchise became at all democratic. This is not surprising, for the job of the liberal state was to maintain and promote the liberal society, which was not essentially a democratic or an equal society. The job of the competitive party system was to uphold the competitive market society, by keeping the government responsive to the shifting majority interests of those who were running the market society.

However, the market society did produce, after a time, a pressure for democracy which became irresistible. Those who had no vote saw that they had no weight in the political market—they had, so to speak, no political purchasing power. Since they had no political purchasing power, their interests were, by the logic of the system, not consulted. When they saw this, they came to demand the vote for themselves, using the general right of association to organize their demand. When they did so, there was, equally in the logic of the system, no defensible ground for withholding the vote from them. For the liberal society had always justified itself as providing equal individual rights and equality of opportunity.

So finally the democratic franchise was introduced into the liberal state. It did not come easily or quickly. In most of the present liberal-democratic countries it required many decades of agitation and organization, and in few countries was anything like it achieved until late in the nineteenth century. The female half of the population had to wait even longer for an equal political voice: not until substantial numbers of women had moved out from the shelter of the home to take an independent place in the labour market was women's claim to a voice in the political market allowed.

So democracy came as a late addition to the competitive market society and the liberal state. The point of recalling this

is, of course, to emphasize that democracy came as an adjunct
to the competitive liberal society and state. It is not simply that
democracy came later. It is also that democracy in these societies,
was demanded, and was admitted, on competitive liberal grounds.
Democracy was demanded, and admitted, on the ground that it
was unfair not to have it in a competitive society. It was something the competitive society logically needed. This is not to say
that all the popular movements whose pressures resulted in the
democratic franchise, and all the writers whose advocacy helped
their cause, were devotees of the market society. But the bulk of
them were. The main demand was for the franchise as the logical
completion of the competitive market society.

In short, by the time democracy came, in the present liberal-
democratic countries, it was no longer opposed to the liberal
society and the liberal state. It was, by then, not an attempt by
the lower class to overthrow the liberal state or the competitive
market economy; it was an attempt by the lower class to take
their fully and fairly competitive place within those institutions
and that system of society. Democracy had been transformed.
From a threat to the liberal state it had become a fulfilment of
the liberal state.

Those who got the franchise did of course increasingly use
their newly-won political voice to demand from the state various
services, in the fields of education, health, and welfare, which
had previously not been provided or provided only scantily. They
used it at the same time to demand a lot of state regulation designed to protect them from the harsher effects, which they had
long felt, of competition between bargainers of unequal economic
power.

Since then, the liberal-democratic state has typically become a
welfare state, and a regulatory state. The rise of the welfare and
regulatory state is generally held to be the result of the extension
of the franchise. It is also generally held that the welfare and
regulatory state has fundamentally altered the market society.
Both these propositions are much more doubtful than they look.
I shall deal with the second proposition in a later lecture. But
here we may notice that the first proposition, which may seem
self-evident, is in fact very doubtful. It is far from clear that the
welfare and regulatory state came because of the democratic
franchise.

It is true that the liberal-democratic state provides a good many services, and does a good deal of planning and controlling, that the nineteenth-century liberal state—the pre-democratic liberal state—didn't do. But even if the liberal state had not become democratic, it would have had to do these things anyway. For one thing, the capitalist economy has turned out to need a lot of regulation and control to keep it on an even keel. This is so for technical economic reasons which have nothing to do with the democratic franchise, reasons which were only fully appreciated by economists and by governments after the great depression of the 1930s. Equally, the extensive provision of social services would have come anyway, apart from the democratic franchise. It would have come from the sheer need of governments to allay working-class discontents that were dangerous to the stability of the state. It was Bismarck, the conservative Chancellor of Imperial Germany, and no great democrat, who pioneered the welfare state in the 1880s, for just this purpose.

What the addition of democracy to the liberal state did was simply to provide constitutional channels for popular pressures, pressures to which governments would have had to yield in about the same measure anyway, merely to maintain public order and avoid revolution. By admitting the mass of the people into the competitive party system, the liberal state did not abandon its fundamental nature; it simply opened the competitive political system to all the individuals who had been created by the competitive market society. The liberal state fulfilled its own logic. In so doing, it neither destroyed nor weakened itself; it strengthened both itself and the market society. It liberalized democracy while democratizing liberalism.

Non-liberal Democracy: the
2 **Communist Variant**

We in the West have achieved a unique political system, a combination of liberal state and democratic franchise. But we should not appropriate for it a title—democracy—which not only used to have a very different meaning, but which also now has a different meaning in the whole non-Western world. When we mean liberal-democracy we should say liberal-democracy.

What then is non-liberal democracy? I said in my first lecture that democracy was originally a class affair. It meant rule by or in the interests of the hitherto oppressed class. It is in something like this sense that democracy has been and is understood by the revolutionary movements which have come to power both in the present Soviet countries and in the newly-independent nations of Africa and Asia. I say, in something *like* this old class sense. But not precisely and entirely in the class sense. For, as I have said, the meaning of democracy has changed in these non-liberal countries too. It has changed from a primarily class concept to a humanistic concept transcending class. Let us see how this has happened.

We may begin by noticing that, even when democracy appeared to be most completely a class concept, it was more than that. Democracy appeared as a class thing mostly to upper-class eyes.

It was mainly ruling-class spokesmen, who had always thought
and spoken in terms of class politics, who treated the claims of
the democrats as class claims. The ruling class has always had
a clearer notion of class politics than the democrats have had.
To the people at the bottom, or even half-way up, democracy
was never entirely or essentially a class thing. For them it had
always been not just a way of freeing themselves from oppression,
but of freeing the whole of humanity, of permitting the realization of the humanity of all men. It was, for them, a class thing
only insofar as they saw the existing ruling class as *the* obstacle
to human fulfilment. If they were, or appeared to be, class-
centred, this was because in the circumstances that was the only
way they could see to be humanity-centred.

In the circumstances, they cannot be blamed. Where the ever-
present and overriding fact was class rule, or a foreign rule
which kept virtually all of a colonial people in the position of a
lower class, the people at the bottom were apt to see this not just
as the oppression of a class, but as an affront to their humanity,
and so as an affront to humanity as such.

This has been so most notably in the communist concept of
democracy, which has always been more of a class concept than
the newer revolutionary democratic concepts which now flourish
in the non-communist underdeveloped nations. For the sake of
clarity we had better consider these two brands of non-liberal
democracy separately. I shall take the rest of this lecture to consider the communist one.

The communist theory goes back of course to the work of Karl
Marx from the 1840s to the 1880s. Two things about it are
important for us to notice. First, it was from the beginning a
highly moralistic theory. In spite of its cold analytical structure
—and compared with most of the rival socialist theories it was
remarkably objective—it had a strong ethical content. The driving force of Marx's whole thought was the belief that man had it
in him to be a freely creative being. With this went the belief
that although throughout history (and pre-history) man had so
far been unable (for quite specific reasons) to realize his full
human nature, now for the first time the conditions for his doing
so were within sight. The reasons it had been impossible were
simply that the level of material productivity had always been so

low that the bulk of mankind was condemned to compulsive labour, and that, to organize this labour, a more or less oppressive ruling class had always been needed. The reason that this was no longer necessary was that capitalism—the last of the many class-divided systems of production—had brought into being such tremendous productive capacities, far exceeding those of any previous system, that now for the first time the release of mankind from compulsive labour was becoming technically possible. With his release from compulsive labour, and from the oppression of a class-divided society, man could become fully human for the first time. This was Marx's humanistic vision, the first of the two things I have said it was important for us to see.

What did this entail by way of political systems? This brings us to the second thing we must notice: the role Marx assigned to class political action and class political structure in the change to the ultimate good society.

The capitalist society that Marx saw was a sharply class-divided one, and on his analysis class exploitation was an essential part of the capitalist system. So long as the capitalist system existed, the state was bound to be an apparatus of force by which one class maintained its power to exploit the others. Capitalism therefore had to go: only the productive powers it had developed were to be kept. It followed that the capitalist state would have to be overthrown before class exploitation could be ended and humanity freed to realize its full potential. The agent for this overthrow, Marx argued, could be none other than the exploited working-class, the politically conscious proletariat. They would have to take over the political power, and use it to transform all the power relations of the capitalist system, substituting social ownership and control of production for private capitalist ownership and control. They would thus establish the political rule of the proletariat, a rule which would be just as powerful as the previous class rule of the capitalists. Marx used the term dictatorship for both. Dictatorship of the proletariat would replace dictatorship of the capitalists, and would last as long as was necessary to transform the society from capitalist to socialist.

This period of proletarian rule Marx called democracy. We are so used to thinking of dictatorship and democracy as opposites that to call this democracy strikes us as outrageous. To call

it liberal-democracy would be outrageous, for there was intended
to be nothing liberal about it. But to call it democracy was not
outrageous at all: it was simply to use the word in its original
and then normal sense. This was Marx's meaning when he wrote
in the Communist Manifesto of 1848, that "the first step in the
revolution by the working class, is to raise the proletariat to the
position of ruling class, to win the battle of democracy". Democracy was to be a class state; it was to use its power to abolish the
legal basis of capitalism and put the productive powers of the
whole society, including all its accumulated capital, at the service
of the whole society.

But the point of all this was that this class state was to be only
a first step. The class division between proletariat and capitalist
was, in Marx's view, the last historically necessary form of class
division. When the proletarian state had abolished the capitalist
order, society would no longer have to consist of opposed classes.
Classes, in the old exploitive sense, would disappear, and so
would the class state. So democracy, for Marx, would be a class
state with a difference, for its whole purpose would be to establish a classless society and so bring to an end the era of class
states.

The Marxian idea of democracy, in short, started from the
age-old notion of democracy as class rule but gave it a new turn
by making it more precise. The old notion had been rather vague
about how the liberation of a class was to be the liberation of
humanity. Marx gave it a new precision by relating it to the historical development of systems of production, and particularly of
the capitalist system of production. The working class created by
capitalism could liberate itself by taking political power. Its rule
would be democratic because it would comprise the great majority of the population, and because its purpose would be the
humanization of the whole people. This democracy would be
class rule at first, for class rule was needed to transform the
capitalist economy to a socialist economy. When the economic
transformation was completed, and abundance for all was attained, there would be no more need for class rule. Thus the
liberation of a class would lead to the humanization of the whole
society by definite stages, starting with the taking of power by
a mass proletariat.

As everyone knows, things did not work out exactly as Marx had expected. The working-class, in the most advanced capitalist countries, as they became conscious of their political strength and got an effective political voice, used that voice not to reject, but to improve their place in, the capitalist system. Proletarian revolution, when it came, came in a country in which capitalism had only been going for a few decades, and in which the proletariat was still a relatively small island in a sea of peasants.

It was apparent to Lenin, who was to lead the Russian revolution in 1917, that something had gone wrong with Marx's timetable. Lenin believed, as firmly as Marx had done, that capitalism was doomed, and that the only way ahead was through a proletarian revolution and a transitional democratic dictatorship of the proletariat, leading ultimately to a classless society. But he concluded that the working-class by itself, under conditions of capitalism, was spontaneously capable only of what he called trade-union consciousness.

What then was to be done? As early as 1902, Lenin argued that the proletarian revolution would have to be the work of what he called a vanguard, a fully class-conscious minority. If and when the vanguard could make a revolution they could bring the rest of the working-class along. The opportunity for such a revolution came in Russia in October 1917, when the constitutional liberal-capitalist government, which had inherited power from the defunct Tsarist régime a few months earlier, was showing itself incapable of governing the war-torn and class-torn society.

So the first communist revolution was made by a vanguard in the name of a whole class. And the Soviet state was from the beginning run by the vanguard, that is, the tightly-knit centrally-controlled Communist Party. Its objectives were the Marxian objectives, to use state power to transform the society from a capitalist to a classless society. But instead of the material basis being present at the time of the revolution, the material basis had still to be created. Marx had counted on the high productivity and high productive potential of an industrially advanced capitalist system. That was to be the base from which material production could be increased still further under socialism. Without a high level of material production, as he knew, there could be no hope of a classless society. The history of the Soviet state since 1917 has been the history of desperate attempts to make up that lack while seeking to bring the mass of the people into the socialist system as full supporters of it.

From the beginning the leaders saw the need to make the system democratic. You could not rely on a vanguard forever. A vanguard alone could not transform society. Yet if the society were to be transformed, a nation mainly of backward peasants had to be modernized, and a large proportion of the whole labour of the society had to be held back from the production of things for people to eat and use, and put into the production of the capital equipment that was needed if a really high standard of productivity was ever to be achieved.

The Soviet state started, therefore, at one remove from the original Marxian concept of democracy. Instead of being able to start as a class democracy it had to start as a vanguard state. It had to try to work towards a high-productivity classless society while it was making up the distance between the vanguard state and that full proletarian democracy which Marx had envisaged as the first stage immediately after the revolution.

We cannot here attempt to follow through all the changes in the political theory and practice of the Soviets as the world situation changed and as they tried one expedient after another. Materially, they now seem to be within sight of their goal of a classless society. For a long time the prevailing Western opinion was that the leaders had lost sight of the goal. This opinion is now changing. For it is now clear that even if there were nothing at stake but the continued maintenance of the Soviet system, and the maintenance of its leaders in positions of power, they would be compelled to move towards the original goal. For with the new stage that military technology has reached, the Soviet system can only hope to make its way in the world, or even hold its place in the world, by influence rather than by might. And its influence, both within the working class in advanced countries, and in the underdeveloped nations of Asia and Africa, depends entirely on the progress it can make towards the goal of a classless society.

These facts, increasingly realized in the West, have gone some way to revising the view that was fashionable until a few years ago, that the Soviet system was simply a despotism exercised by the few leaders of an élite party over the whole mass of the Soviet people. But the question we have to consider is whether a vanguard state can properly be considered democratic, even in the classic non-liberal sense of democracy. There can be no simple answer to this question. The answer depends, ultimately, on whether you consider democracy to be a system of government only, or whether you take it to be a kind of society.

If you take it in the narrow or strict sense to be a system of government, then you must use it to mean only a system in which the majority actually controls the rulers, actually controls those who make and enforce political decisions. Obviously, the majority itself cannot continuously rule, in any society larger than a town meeting, but democracy surely requires that the majority should really control those who do rule.

Even this formula is not at all clear. How much control is real control? Where, in the whole spectrum of possible degrees of control, do you draw the line? Must every official from highest to lowest be directly elected and be held annually, or daily, accountable? Must they all be simply instructed delegates of their constituents, not allowed to exercise any independent judgment? This would be real control, but it might well make it impossible to carry on the business of government at all.

Or, at the other extreme, is it enough that all power should emanate from a leader who gets his authority from occasional plebiscites, where the only question is, do you support the leader? We would all say that this is not real control.

The only real and feasible majority control falls somewhere between these extremes. If majority rule is really to mean anything, at least the majority must be able to say what they want, and to make it stick.

But this brings us abruptly up against a basic problem which is inescapable in all revolutionary periods. What makes a period revolutionary is a more or less widespread belief that the existing system of power, the existing system of power relations between people, is somehow thwarting their humanity. This was just as true of the great liberal revolutions, the English revolution of the seventeenth century and the French revolution of the eighteenth century, as it is of the non-liberal revolutions of the twentieth century. If you believe, as the makers of all these revolutions have believed, that the very structure of the society, the dominant power relations in it, have made people less than fully human, have warped them into inability to realize or even to see their full human potentiality, what are you to do? How can the debasing society be changed by those who have themselves been debased by it? This is the problem that has faced not only liberal and radical, but also conservative, reformers, from Plato to Rousseau, from St. Thomas More to Marx. The debased people are, by definition, incapable of reforming themselves *en masse*. They cannot be expected to pull themselves up by their own bootstraps.

The answers that have been given by the greatest political reformers, from the most conservative to the most radical, have relied on a morally or intellectually superior leadership, temporary or permanent. Plato, the most acute thinker of the ancient classical world, came out for permanent authoritarian rule by an intellectual and physical élite group. Rousseau came out for a moral transformation of the people by a leader of the kind sociologists now call charismatic—one whose greatness of soul would create a purified general will capable of sustaining an equal, free and democratic society. Lenin, building on Marx, came out for a seizure of power by a vanguard who would forcibly transform the basic relations of society in such a way that the people would become undebased and capable of a fully human existence, at which point compulsive government would no longer be needed.

Each of these ways is exceedingly dangerous. There can be no guarantee that Plato's authoritarian rulers, or Rousseau's charismatic leader, or Lenin's vanguard, will in fact use their power for the ends for which it was supposed to be used. Yet, in the circumstances we are talking about, there seems to be no less dangerous way. The notion that individual regeneration on a large scale, within the old society, could bring about the desired change, has failed repeatedly. People who have been debased by their society cannot be morally regenerated except by the society being reformed, and this requires political power.

In a revolutionary period, therefore, when a substantial part of the society senses uneasily that it is dehumanized but does not know quite how, or when it is so dehumanized that only a few of the people at most can be expected to see that they are dehumanized, there is no use relying on the free votes of everybody to bring about a fully human society. If it is not done by a vanguard it will not be done at all.

We in the West have the peculiar good fortune of not now having to face this problem, at least not in this stark form. We have been able to coast on the liberal revolutions of the seventeenth and eighteenth centuries, which, we should remind ourselves, were also made by vanguards.

But to come back to the question, can a vanguard state properly be called a democratic state? If democracy is taken in its narrow sense as meaning simply a system of choosing and authorizing governments, then a vanguard state cannot be called democratic. A vanguard state may be a government *for* the people but it is not government *by* the people, or even by the choice of the people. A vanguard state cannot in principle be a democratic state in the narrow sense, since the whole reason for vanguard rule is that the majority of the people are said to be too debased, too impregnated with the ethics and values of the old inhuman society, to be trusted with immediate power.

But a vanguard state can in principle merge into a democratic state in the narrow sense. It can do so when the desires and value-judgments of the bulk of the people have so changed (as a result of the changes in institutions) that the people will freely support the kind of society that the vanguard state has brought into being.

The conversion of a vanguard state into a strictly democratic state can scarcely take place while the post-revolutionary state is still a class state. On this point I think it must be conceded that Lenin was more perceptive than Marx. But in the measure that the old exploitive class system has been overcome, and no new one allowed to take its place, the change can be made.

The change does not necessarily require that a system of competing parties be set up. But if there is only one party, there must be, within it, effective means for those at the bottom to control those at the top. There must be an effective measure of what is called intra-party democracy. All ruling communist parties claim to have this. We in the West think it very doubtful that any of them have it. But Western scholars do see a trend in this direction, although the evidence is so unclear that there is no certainty as to how far the trend has gone. But it is well to notice that the trend can in principle go on without any overt change in the political system.

It may still be said that a one-party state, even with the fullest intra-party democracy, cannot strictly be called democratic in the narrow sense. For no matter how full the intra-party democracy, and no matter how open the party membership, this still gives an effective voice only to those who are politically active enough to be members of the party. And in all communist states up to the present, membership in the party has generally required much more strenuous activity than most people in those countries are prepared to give. Most of us would say that this degree of strenuous activity is too high a price to pay for a political voice, and that a system that sets so high a price cannot be called democratic. Yet how many of us would say that there should be no price at all, that everyone, whether or not he stirs himself politically at all, should have an effective political voice? If we allow that some minimum degree of activity should be a requirement for having a political voice, then a single-party system which does not demand inordinate activity can qualify as democratic. To qualify as such, membership in the party must be wide open: otherwise, some would be denied the right to an effective voice.

It appears, then, that a one-party state can in principle be democratic even in the narrow sense, provided (1) that there is full intra-party democracy, (2) that party membership is open, and (3) that the price of participation in the party is not a greater degree of activity than the average person can reasonably be expected to contribute. The first two conditions can scarcely be met until the old class society has been replaced; the third condition we can expect will take a little longer to be met. It does not appear that these three conditions have as yet been met in any communist states, although it must be admitted that we cannot state the conditions in such a precise way as to enable their fulfilment or non-fulfilment to be tested quantitatively.

We began with the question whether a vanguard state on the Leninist model could be called a democratic system of government. I answered, no, and went on to consider on what conditions vanguard rule could change into effectively democratic rule, still within a one-party system. I have stated the conditions, and they do not appear to have been met.

But we must recall that these are the conditions which have to be met only if democracy in the narrow sense is to be properly claimed. And we must notice that, besides this narrow sense of democracy, there is a broader sense which, historically speaking, is equally legitimate. Democracy has very generally been taken to mean something more than a system of government. Democracy in this broader sense has always contained an ideal of human equality, not just equality of opportunity to climb a class ladder, but such an equality as could only be fully realized in a society where no class was able to dominate or live at the expense of others.

If this broader concept of democracy as equality is admitted, the claims of a vanguard state appear in a different light. Wherever the circumstances are such that no motion towards this kind of society is possible except through the action of a vanguard, then the vanguard state, so long as it remains true to its purpose, may be called democratic.

Communist states have generally claimed to be democratic in both the narrow and the broader sense. This I think has been a mistake. They would have done better, if they valued the opinion of the West, to claim to be democratic only in the broader sense: they would then more easily be believed when they reached the point where they could properly claim it in the narrow governmental sense as well. But when the communist states started, they were not much interested in the good opinion of the West, for the prospect of it was utterly remote. Now, when strong new reasons have made peaceful co-existence a necessity, the prospect of that good opinion is suddenly much closer. And so the damage that has been done by their past democratic claims appears serious. It can only be repaired in the measure that the communist states can make good their claim to be democratic in the narrow sense. Fortunately, the new international climate of co-existence is making it easier for them to move in this direction.

Non-liberal Democracy: the
3   Underdeveloped Variant

Everyone recognizes that a new world has emerged in Africa and Asia in our own time—the third world, as it is sometimes called, of newly-independent underdeveloped countries. This third world, neither communist nor capitalist, now comprises most of Africa and, except for China and the fragmentary states of North Korea and North Viet Nam, virtually all of South and East Asia. The peoples of this new world have achieved independence from colonial rule within the last ten or twenty years. Some got their independence only after a revolutionary struggle; others got theirs without an actual show of force. Either way, the change was so great that it may properly be called a revolution. These revolutions characteristically are made by an organized popular movement under leaders who are able to get mass support for their vision of the future. A part, if not the whole, of that vision has generally been a vision of democracy.

What does this vision of democracy amount to? It is different from both the concepts of democracy we have looked at so far. It is neither our Western liberal-democracy nor the democracy formulated by Marx and Lenin. It is newer than either of these, yet in a sense it is older than both, for it seems to go directly back to the old notion of democracy, which pre-dates Marx and pre-dates the liberal state, the notion of democracy as rule by and for the oppressed people. Since the underdeveloped nations had on the whole a simpler culture than those who had dominated them, it is not surprising that they resorted to a concept of democracy that goes back to a simpler pre-industrial society.

We saw in the first lecture how this original notion of democracy had, in the West, been transformed before and while being admitted into the liberal state to become liberal-democracy. We saw in the second lecture how the original notion had been changed in a different way in the communist theory. Marx and Lenin had given democracy a specific class content, and had seen class democracy becoming a fully human society in two successive stages of development. The notion of democracy that has emerged in the underdeveloped countries, in the course of their drive for national independence from colonialism, is closer to the original notion than are either of the others. It had not been transformed by liberal-individualism, nor made over on the definite class pattern of Marxism.

Perhaps the best way to see what it is, is to look at what the new nations have typically rejected and accepted in both the liberal and the Marxian theories. This is the way the under-developed new nations have come at it themselves, for most of the new leaders have been educated in the West, or at least in the European tradition; they are generally familiar with both liberal and Marxian theory, and have arrived at their own theory by conscious selection of those elements in both theories which they have thought applicable to the problems, present and future, of their own people. And if we look not only at *what* they have rejected and accepted, but also *why*, we shall perhaps be able to judge how firmly based their theories are, and how lasting they are likely to be.

It has to be said at once that the underdeveloped countries have on the whole rejected the most characteristic features of liberal-democracy. That their concept of democracy is not liberal-individualist is not surprising. It would be surprising if it were. The competitive market society, which is the soil in which liberal ideas and the liberal state flourish, was not natural to them. Insofar as they knew the market society, it was something imposed on them from outside and from above. Their traditional culture was generally not attuned to competition. They generally saw no intrinsic value in wealth-getting and gave no respect to the motive of individual gain. Equality and community, equality within a community, were traditionally rated more highly than individual freedom.

The notion of political competition was just as unnatural to them as the notion of economic competition, so that there was little basis for a system of competing political parties. There were, and still are, in some of these countries, tribal or religious or ethnic divisions which have stood in the way of an overriding sense of national community. These divisions have sometimes given rise to opposed political parties. But the notion that a system of competing national parties is the sensible and most beneficial way of choosing and authorizing governments is something quite foreign to these countries.

Not only has there been no traditional base for a market society or a liberal state, but also there has been nothing to encourage a liberal development in the years of the independence movement and of the immediate post-independence state. On the contrary, the requirements of the struggle for independence generally favoured the emergence of a dominant single party or mass movement. This has in most cases been carried into the post-independence structure as a one-party system, or at least as what is called a system of single-party-dominance, where one party has an overwhelming legislative majority and uses its legal and political and police powers to restrict the competition of other parties.

The dominance of a single party or movement is, of course, apt to be the immediate aftermath of any revolution. When the revolution is made by a people largely united in a single over-riding will to throw off foreign control, the dominance of a single party is even more likely. When the people who are so united were not sharply class-divided among themselves, the single-party pattern is still more likely. And when, finally, their goal is not only to attain independence but thereafter to modernize the society, and to raise very substantially the level of material productivity, the one-party system is almost irresistible.

There is no doubt that the new underdeveloped nations have to modernize and raise their productivity, in order to keep their

independence, let alone to make possible a decent human life. In
the underdeveloped countries, this is an enormous job, demand-
ing strong political leadership. There may be, as there commonly
is in these countries, a fairly general will for independence and
even for modernization. But even the strongest general will for
these things needs to be harnessed and to be continually regenerated. It is not inconceivable that this could be done by a liberal
competitive party system, but it is more natural for it to be done
by a single dominant party which has already shown its capacity
to evoke and sustain the necessary general will.

The very enormity of the tasks confronting such a new state
is apt to operate in two ways to reinforce the tendency to a non-
liberal state. If the magnitude of the tasks captures the imagination of the whole people, or the whole active part of the people,
they are likely to give full support to the leader and the movement which launched the new state, and are likely to see no point
in competing parties.

But equally, if the magnitude of the tasks fails to enlist the
active support of the whole people, it works in the same direction.
Suppose that there are sections of the population who do not
share this zeal for modernization. Or suppose, as happens often
enough, that there are sections who share the general purpose but
who, because of tribal or religious or language differences, are
reluctant to work under the leadership of the dominant party,
and who consequently seek to establish or maintain opposition
movements or parties. In such cases, their opposition is apt to be
regarded as close to treason. For the newly-independent nation
has to work, if not to fight, for its very life. It is bound to press
on with the work of modernization at the risk of falling again
under outside domination. The fear of falling into what they call
neo-colonialism is always present. Hence, opposition to the
dominant party appears to be, and sometimes actually is, destruc-
tive of the chances of nationhood. In such circumstances opposition appears as treason against the nation. Matters are made
worse if there is evidence, as there sometimes is, that the opposition has placed itself at the service of the foreigner, but this is
not needed to make opposition appear as treason.

Thus in a newly-independent underdeveloped country there
are strong inherent pressures against a liberal-democratic system.

The pressures militate not only against a competitive party system but also against the maintenance of realistic civil liberties. Freedom of speech and publication, and freedom from arbitrary arrest and detention, are under the same sort of pressure as is freedom of association.

This pressure for an illiberal state is apt to last longer in these countries than was the case in the classic liberal revolutions of the seventeenth and eighteenth centuries (which were illiberal enough for a decade or two). For there are two factors present in these new revolutions which were absent in the earlier liberal ones. One is the need to accumulate large amounts of capital for economic development. In the classic liberal revolutions, the capital, and the capitalist enterprise and skill, were there, in the country, ready and anxious to go ahead. In the present revolutions this is not so: there must therefore be a painful, long period of accumulation of capital and of productive skills. The other factor is the need to create a pervasive loyalty to the nation rather than to the tribe, the ethnic community or the local community. A pre-political and pre-national people has to be brought to a political and national consciousness. This puts a premium on the mass movement with strong ideological leadership. This factor was not present in anything like the same degree in the classic liberal revolutions, which did not generally occur until after a nation had been molded by other centralizing forces.

For all these reasons, the prevalence of non-liberal political systems in the newly-independent underdeveloped countries is not surprising. But what of their claim to be democratic?

This claim rests largely on the proposition that there is in these countries a general will, which can express itself through, and probably only through, a single party. That there is more nearly a single general will in these countries than in the more competitive, more individualized, and more class-stratified societies of the West, must, I think, be allowed. Whether the expression of this will through a single party can be called democratic in the strict sense depends on how much control there is of the leaders by the rank-and-file within the party, that is, how much intra-party democracy there is, and beyond that, on how open membership in the party is, and how strenuous a degree of activity is required as the price of membership in the party.

I gave reasons in the second lecture for thinking that a one-party system may properly be called democratic only if there is full intra-party democracy, if party membership is open, and if the price of participation in the party is not a greater degree of activity than the average person can reasonably be expected to contribute. These I said were the conditions that had to be met before a vanguard state could become a democratic state. I also pointed out that these conditions were unlikely to be met while the post-revolutionary state was still a class state.

So far as one can generalize about all the new underdeveloped nations, I think one can say that these conditions are more nearly met there than in the communist countries. And this is what we should expect, since in these new nations the revolutions have not generally been class revolutions, and the new states not generally class states.

The new states were indeed brought into existence by mass movements headed by a strong vanguard, but the vanguard was not generally as separated from the mass as it was in the communist revolutions. It was not so separated because the class circumstances were different. In the communist revolutions, as we saw, the typical situation was a small industrial working class, of which only a still smaller minority was highly class-conscious, in a surrounding sea of peasants. The vanguard was separated from the rest in two ways. It was separated from the rest of the industrial working-class by its degree of class-consciousness and from the mass of the people by its different class basis—the vanguard being based on wage-workers rather than peasants.

In the new revolutions the typical situation has been different. The vanguard has been distinguished from the mass much more largely by degree of political consciousness only, not by being from a different class. And the political consciousness of the vanguard has been national rather than class consciousness. The vanguard has typically been at one remove, rather than two removes, from the mass of the peasantry, the one remove being in educational advantage, zeal, and ability, more than anything else. They can therefore properly claim to represent a general will more fully, or at least more immediately after the revolution, than where the vanguard was more separate from the mass. Even so, as we have noticed, they cannot automatically be assumed to have the whole nation behind them from the beginning. Yet where there is a relatively classless general will for certain great objectives like national independence and economic growth, where this will is originally stronger in each person than any divergent wills for subsidiary objects, and where this will has to be *kept* stronger through a long and sacrificial period of capital accumulation and structural reorganization, and can only be kept strong by drawing more people more actively into conscious political life, there the political system which can best do this may not improperly be called democratic.

To call it democratic is to put the emphasis on ends, not means. It is to make the criterion of democracy the achievement of ends which the mass of the people share and which they put ahead of separate individual ends. And this of course is the classic, pre-liberal, notion of democracy. The classic formulator of this democratic doctrine was Rousseau, and there are strong echoes of Rousseau in many of the theoretical statements made by leaders in the underdeveloped countries. Like Rousseau, they find the source of their social ills, of moral depravity, of dehumanization and loss of human freedom, in the institution of inequality. Like him they believe that men can be restored to full freedom and humanity by, and only by, the operation of a general will. Dignity, freedom, and humanity are to be achieved by re-establishing the equality that had been forcibly or fraudulently taken from them. This requires a revolution at once political and moral, an assertion of the will of an undifferentiated people as the only legitimate source of political power.

The basic moral assertion made by this doctrine is the ultimate worth of the dignity and freedom of the human being. This is what the classic democratic doctrine has in common with the liberal doctrine. Where they differ is in their practical assertions. The classic doctrine asserts that this end can only be achieved by the operation of an undifferentiated general will. And the democratic doctrine of the underdeveloped countries is the classic doctrine.

We conclude, then, that the new underdeveloped nations have on the whole a genuine claim to be called democratic, though not liberal-democratic. They have rejected the most characteristic features of liberal-democracy, and have done so for reasons that are likely to persist. The one thing they have in common with liberal-democracy is the ultimate ideal of a life of freedom and dignity and moral worth for every member of the society.

We may now look at what the underdeveloped countries have accepted and rejected in the Marxian concept of democracy. The main thing they have rejected, for reasons which we have already glimpsed, is the class analysis. I shall look at this more closely in a moment, but perhaps first we might notice what those of them who have been most affected by Marxism have taken from the Marxian theory.

What they have found congenial in Marxism is its general critical analysis of capitalist society, and the moral basis from which that criticism was made. Marx speaks to them directly when he speaks of the dehumanization of man by capitalism. His analysis of the alienation of man, that is, of the spiriting away of man's essential nature by the necessary relations of capitalism, speaks immediately to their own experience, and seems to them to go to the heart of the matter. Equally attractive is Marx's belief that man can remake himself, can overcome his dehumanization, by concerted revolutionary action. But here the attractiveness of Marxism ends.

They do not accept as applicable to their countries the Marxian theory of class struggle as the motive force of history. Nor do they accept Marx's proposition that the state is necessarily an instrument of class domination, or his conclusion that the system of political power which follows immediately after the anti-capitalist revolution must be as much a class state as any preceding one. They do not agree that the way to a classless society must be through a class state.

They may agree that these propositions are valid for developed capitalist societies, but they find them invalid for their own countries. These propositions do not fit their reading of their own experience. For they see their own societies as virtually classless already. Instead of the Marxian pattern of a society internally divided into exploiting and exploited classes, they see a society all of which has been subordinated to an external exploiting power. They see themselves indeed as having been subjugated by capitalism, but it is their whole people, not just one class, that they see as subjugated. Capitalism, imposed on them from outside, has produced within the society not a sharper class division but a relatively classless society.

So their revolution against capitalism is seen as a national revolution rather than a class revolution. Or, if you like, since they see their whole people as having been reduced to one subordinate class, their revolution is at once a class revolution and a national revolution. In freeing themselves from capitalism by throwing off imperial domination, they see themselves freed *immediately* from the whole class system of political power. They see no need, consequently, to go through a period of a class state after the revolution. They find no need for a dictatorship of the proletariat. As soon as the imperial power has been driven out, there is no strong indigenous capitalist class that needs to be suppressed by a proletarian state. What they find they require, therefore, is not a dictatorship of a proletariat (or of a vanguard in the name of a proletariat) but the dictatorship of a general will (or of a vanguard in the name of the general will) over an undifferentiated people.

These conclusions, drawn from their own reading of their own situation, are in most cases close enough to reality to confirm the newly-independent colonial countries in their non-communist position. Communist doctrine and communist movements can take hold only where there is something for them to take hold of. What they need is a situation of class opposition within the country. The doctrine was, after all, worked out to deal with countries where there was a real internal conflict of classes, or where forces making for such a conflict were thought to be present. So the doctrine is not clearly and directly applicable to the underdeveloped countries, in which there are few or no exploitive class divisions once the foreign rule has been ended.

But we must notice that something approximating this internal class conflict can be created by the action of outside powers, as in the Congo and in Viet Nam. Wherever an outside power has succeeded, during or immediately after a revolution for independence, in getting one part of the popular movement (or one of two popular movements) to follow its policy, but where this does not stem the tide of the independence movement, the result is civil war. And it is a civil war which appears at the same time to be an internal class war. For a civil war, no matter how much one side is assisted or sustained by a foreign power, is an internal conflict. And this kind of civil war appears, to one side at least, as a conflict between those who are determined to drive out the foreign power, which to them represents exploitive capitalism, and those who have come to terms with the foreigner and hence with exploitive capitalism. This makes it in effect an internal *class* conflict. Class lines which were not present originally have, so to speak, been imposed from outside.

So where a civil war of this kind develops, the Marxian class analysis appears, to one side, to be applicable, and the communist doctrine is readily received. But this is the exceptional case. More usually the independence movement has expelled the foreigners decisively enough that the class analysis is inapplicable.

I have sketched rather rapidly the ways in which the concept of democracy in the newly-independent underdeveloped countries differs both from the liberal and the communist concepts. I have looked at the claim of these new single-party or single-party-dominance states to be democratic, both in the narrow governmental sense and in the broader social sense. I have suggested that they have a claim on both counts.

Their claim to be democratic in the narrow sense is I think somewhat better than that of the communist states, since they are more nearly able to meet the three conditions which must be met if a one-party state is to be democratic in the governmental sense. The three conditions, you will recall, were that there be some real control from the bottom within the party, that party membership be open, and that the degree of political activity demanded of party members be not more than the average person will steadily give.

The reason these conditions can be expected to be met more readily in the former colonial countries than in the communist countries is that in the colonial countries there generally has been, at the time of the revolution, relatively little internal class division of an exploitive kind. So, by comparison with the communist states, there has generally been no need of a class state after the revolution. And it is the existence of a class state that stands most in the way of our three conditions being met, for a post-revolutionary class state has to suppress the old ruling class and all manifestations of the old way of life while trying to transform the society.

The underdeveloped countries' claim to be democratic in the broader sense may also, though more doubtfully, be thought to be a little better than the communist claim. To be democratic in the broader sense means to be moving towards a firmly-held goal of an equal society in which everybody can be fully human. What gives the new underdeveloped nations the advantage on this count is their relative classlessness. Not having to go through a period of dictatorship of the proletariat, they can begin immediately on what might be called a classless struggle with nature, a concerted effort to raise the standard of life, an effort in which all can participate with a sense of equality.

Yet this advantage is offset by a clear disadvantage. The underdeveloped nations have a lot farther to go than the European communist countries before they can reach a level of material productivity that begins to make possible a fully human life for everybody. Democracy in the broad sense requires not just equality but also freedom from starvation, ignorance, and early diseased death. If the communist countries and the new underdeveloped nations both hold to their goal of an equal, non-exploitive, and in that sense democratic society, the former will presumably reach the goal sooner than the latter. How much of the way they will travel democratically cannot be predicted with any assurance.

But it is perhaps less useful to try to compare the democratic claims of the communist and the underdeveloped countries, than simply to see that they both have claims, and that the claims are based largely on the classic notion of democracy as an equal human society.

More important still is to see the strength of the forces that are likely to hold them on a path different from liberal-democracy. Liberal-democracy is the politics of choice. Everything is up for choice, or may be up for choice at any time—everything, that is to say, except the liberal society and the democratic franchise themselves. The ideal of liberal-democracy is consumers' sovereignty—we buy what we want with our votes. An underdeveloped country cannot afford this kind of political consumers' sovereignty: it has too few political goods to offer. Once an underdeveloped people has taken the decision to become an independent nation, it is committed to a course of action which severely limits the range of further choices. The power of the state *must* be used to push the economic development of the country at a rather forced pace if national independence is to be kept. Once the one big choice is made, it stands in the way of that continuous flow of lesser choices which is the characteristic feature of the liberal state. The new states cannot afford the politics of extreme choice. We in the West treat government itself as a consumers' good; they have to treat it as a producers' good, a capital investment. And like all capital investments it cannot be controlled directly, but at most only indirectly and at one long remove, by consumer choices.

Liberal-Democracy as a System of Power

4

Our investigation so far has shown us that there are three concepts of democracy actively at work in the world today, each one shaping and being shaped by a particular kind of society at a particular stage of development. There is our Western liberal-democracy, which we saw was brought into being to serve the needs of the competitive market society. Liberal-democracy is a fairly late product of the market society; the first need of the market society was for the liberal state, not a democratic one: a liberal state which was designed to operate by competition between political parties responsible to a non-democratic electorate. The democratic franchise was added only when the working-class that had been produced by the capitalist market society had become strong enough to get into the competition, strong enough to demand that it should have some weight in the competitive process. Liberal-democracy is thus the unique product of successfully developing capitalist market societies.

We have seen also the two non-liberal kinds of democracy, both of them closer than ours to the original notion of democracy as rule by and for the poor and oppressed, a notion that had nothing liberal about it. The modern communist concept, we saw, took the old notion and made it more precise and schematic by reading into it a specific class content and a specific time scheme. Democracy, for Marx and Lenin, meant in the first instance, rule by or for the proletariat. It was a class state, to be created by proletarian revolution, and to have the job of holding down the old ruling class while transforming the whole society in such a way that there would be no more basis for exploitive classes and so no more need for a class state. Only then could class democracy give way to a fully human society.

We saw, finally, a third concept of democracy, neither liberal nor communist, which prevails in the third world of the newly-independent underdeveloped countries. It rejects the competitive ethos of the market society and sees no need for the competitive system of political parties. But while it thus adopts the pattern of the one-party state, it rejects the communist idea that where a people has broken away from capitalism the post-revolutionary state must be a class state. It sees instead the possibility of operating immediately as a classless society and state. Democracy, in this view, becomes immediately rule by the general will: this starts the moment national independence is attained.

The real world of democracy consists of all these three kinds, not just of any one of them. It is just as unrealistic for us to assume that ours is the only true democracy as it is for the Soviets or the third world to insist that theirs is the only genuine kind. The three kinds are indeed so different that one might ask whether one word should properly be used to describe them all. Can three such different animals really be given the same name? The simplest answer is that they are in fact given the same name. To this one might object, of course, that the Communists and the third world have simply pounced on a good Western word when they saw it, and have appropriated it to their own systems for public relations purposes. This seems to be the view of a good many of our newspaper writers and publicists, who are perhaps more familiar with public relations than with democracy. But this view, as we have seen, is quite false. The idea of democracy goes a long way farther back than the period of liberal-democracy, and the modern non-liberal notions of democracy are plainly drawn from that original notion.

And when all three concepts of democracy are seen in perspective another reason appears why they should share a single name. They have one thing in common: their ultimate goal is the same

—to provide the conditions for the full and free development of the essential human capacities of all the members of the society. They differ in their views as to what conditions are needed, and as to how they must move to achieve those conditions. And those who live in one system commonly judge that the other systems are going about it in an impossible way, or are not going about it at all. These differences of judgments about means commonly obscure the fact that they share the same ultimate moral end.

Now if coping with the real world of democracy were just a question of weighing the three kinds in some static moral scales, we in the West would easily conclude, in a great majority, that the balance comes down heavily in favour of liberal-democracy. But clearly, this is not good enough. It does not cope. For there is the awkward fact that the majority of those in the other two kinds believe that their kind is superior. They do not claim that theirs provide more individual liberty. But they do claim that, while none of the three kinds has yet achieved the democratic moral ideal, they are on the right road and we are at a dead end.

This difference of judgment wouldn't matter too much if each of the three could live and move in isolation from the others. Each could bolster its morale by jumping on and off the moral scales, which it would have adjusted to its own advantage. But clearly the three are not proceeding, and cannot proceed, in isolation. The two most technically advanced sections of our three-way world are competing with each other, each believing that the future is on its side, and each nudging the future in its direction by means which are having serious repercussions on their societies, and indeed on the chances of there being a future at all. We seem to have got over the worst days of the Cold War, but on both sides forces have been set in motion which stand in the way of full and free human development by any road, and which are not easily reversed. We are becoming aware in the West how difficult it is to move away from a war-oriented system, and the fall of Khrushchev suggests that there is a similar difficulty in the Soviet world. Meanwhile the new world of Africa and Asia, under-developed but set on a course of rapid development, is by its mere existence as a third world having effects on the other two. It is in a sense the conscience of the West. It is also a challenge to the Soviets.

So we are in a position rather different from that of the earlier

proponents and defenders of liberal-democracy. We have no
longer just to make an abstract case for liberal-democracy as best
suiting the nature of man. We have to look more critically at
what we used to be able to take for granted. We must do this not
merely to defend ourselves; we must do it to give ourselves an
opportunity of moving from what is now an inadequate basis for
self-satisfaction to a more adequate basis of hope that our vision
of human excellence may prevail.

As soon as we begin to look at this, we see how curiously
limited is the vision of human excellence that has got built into
our society and that we have made do with up to now. It is a
vision that is inextricably linked with the market society. And the
sad truth is that it is a vision of inertia. It is almost incredible,
until you come to think of it, that a society whose keyword is
enterprise, which certainly sounds active, is in fact based on the
assumption that human beings are so inert, so averse to activity,
that is, to expenditure of energy, that every expenditure of energy
is considered to be painful, to be, in the economist's term, a
disutility. This assumption, which is a travesty of the human condition, is built right into the justifying theory of the market
society, and so of the liberal society. The market society, and so
the liberal society, is commonly justified on the grounds that it
maximizes utilities, i.e., that it is the arrangement by which
people can get the satisfactions they want with the least effort.
The notion that activity itself is pleasurable, is a utility, has sunk
almost without a trace under this utilitarian vision of life. This is
not surprising, since the economists, and the liberal theoreticians
following them, have taken as given the capitalist market society
where no one works except for a reward. To see the hollowness
of this vision, one need only ask what we shall all do when
automation, cybernation, and new sources of non-human energy,
have made the system of working for material rewards quite out-
of-date and useless. What then shall we do except expend our
energy in truly human activities—laughing, playing, loving, learning, creating, arranging our lives in ways that give us aesthetic
and emotional satisfaction?

But we must return to the hollow vision, which still domin-
ates our lives, and ask how the rationale of liberal-democracy is
related to it. The first thing we must notice is that liberal-demo-

cracy is, like all other systems of society and government, a system of power.

I said in an earlier lecture that liberal-democracy was the politics of choice. So it is, but it is also a system of power. Indeed, like all other systems of government and of society, it is a double system of power.

Any system of government is a system of power in one obvious sense. Government, by its very nature, is a process whereby rules are made and enforced on individual citizens. Whatever the source of a government's authority, it is empowered to make people do things which some or all of them wouldn't otherwise do, and to prevent people from doing things that some or all of them otherwise would do. If men were angels, government would not be necessary. Since they are not, government is necessary, and government must mean that the governors have power to compel the governed. It is just because this fundamental fact has always been clearly recognized by liberal-democrats that they have always insisted on the governed having some effective control over the governors by way of choice of the governors. It is the mark of a civilized society that private violence be forbidden, and that violence, the power to compel by physical force or constraint, be a monopoly of the government. It is because this kind of power must be a monopoly of the government that we are rightly concerned with controls on the government.

In this sense, then, the most liberal of democrats recognize that the liberal-democratic state, like any other, is a system of power. What is less generally recognized is that liberal-democracy is a system of power in a second sense as well. It, like any other state, exists to maintain a set of relations between individuals and groups within the society which are power relations. This is an unfamiliar idea which will bear some examination.

It would no doubt be foolish to try to reduce all relations between individuals to power relations, though the greatest theorist of modern individualism (I mean Thomas Hobbes, who penetrated to the essentials of our modern market society 300 years ago) had a good shot at it. Not every relation which each of us bears to others can be reduced to a relation of power over others, or of others' power over us. There are relations of love, of friendship, of kinship, of admiration, of common interest, which cannot readily be reduced to relations of power, although there is generally an element of power even in them. Many relations between persons, such as the marriage relation, are a compound of power and non-power relations, and the proportions may change over time. Marriage used to be a chattel relationship, the husband owning the wife; now it is no longer so. The change, we may notice, had to be made by the state. We may say in general that of all relations between people it is only relations of power that fall within the jurisdiction of the state: only those relations need the state to enforce them. It is only power that needs power, only relations involving power that need a superior power to keep them in order. And all the power relations between individuals do need the power of the state to enforce them.

The existence of power relations, and the need of the state to enforce them, is easily seen in kinds of society other than the free market society. In a society where some of the population are slaves, no one doubts that the relation between master and slave is a power relation, or that the state is there to enforce that relation. Similarly, in any society where the whole work of the society is authoritatively allocated to people in different quantities, and where the whole product is authoritatively distributed between them in a way that does not correspond to the different contributions they have made, it is easy to see that there is a power relation between people, which is being enforced by the state. In such a society, some men are getting the benefit of some part of the powers of other men.

These kinds of power relation between individuals are, we may notice, maintained and enforced by way of some legal institution of property. Human beings themselves may be made the legal property of others, as is the case with the institution of slavery. But it is not necessary to go this far in order to ensure that some men will have power over others, in the sense of being able to transfer some of the natural powers of others to themselves. It is quite enough that some rank or class of men should have the sole legal right to property in those things without access to which no man can use his natural powers. Thus if all property in land is held by some superior ranks, as in the feudal system, the inferior ranks are compelled to serve them on whatever terms the superiors set. For in a predominantly agricultural society, a man without access to the land has nothing to work *on*, nothing on which he can work to make a living. A man's natural powers consist at least of his capacities, his strength and skill. But these cannot actually be exerted without something to exert them on. A man's powers, that is to say, cannot be made actual, cannot be used, unless he has access to something he can use them on. A man must have access to the means of labour.

So in any society where the legal institutions give all the property in land, or any other means of labour, to one section of the people, all the others must pay for access to the means of labour. The payment may take the form of compulsory labour— so many days' work a month on the lord's land—or it may be handing over so much of the produce a man has raised on the land which he is allowed to work on that condition, or it may be a money rent. Whatever form the payment takes, it is a transfer of part of a man's powers (or part of the produce of these powers) to another man, and it is compulsive.

This kind of power relationship, by which some are able to transfer part of the powers of others to themselves by virtue of having got a monopoly of the means of labour, is easily enough seen in societies where the ownership of the means of labour is legally restricted to certain ranks or classes. It was in protest against just this kind of power relation that the great liberal revolutions of the seventeenth and eighteenth centuries were made.

The liberal revolutions destroyed that system of property, and set up the kind of state I am calling the liberal state to ensure that there should be no such legal restrictions on ownership of the means of labour. From that time on, all individuals have been free to acquire by their own exertions enough land or capital to work on themselves, or to bargain in the open market for the best price they can get for the use of their labour. So long as competition is free, the market gives everyone exactly what his contribution to production is worth. And the market does this quite impersonally, through a mechanism of free contracts and freely-made bargains between individuals. The job of the liberal state is simply to protect and enforce the mechanism of free contract, and to ensure each the right to such property as he can acquire by his labour and by his contracts.

This is a far cry from the compulsion exercised by earlier, non-liberal states. The liberal state does indeed use power to enforce a system of relations between individuals, but the relations it enforces do not themselves appear to be compulsive. They do not appear to be relations by which some people are enabled to transfer part of the powers of others to themselves. How then can we say that the liberal state, guaranteeing the market society, is a double system of power, as much so as were the earlier states which guaranteed a clearly compulsive transfer of powers? For a system of government is a double system of power only when the relations between individuals which it enforces are themselves power relations. And we have taken these power relations to mean relations by which some men are able to get more out of others than others get out of them, or to get a net transfer of some of the powers of others to themselves.

What has to be shown, then, before we can call the liberal state a double system of power, is that the capitalist market society which it upholds is a system of net transfer of some men's powers to other men. It is not difficult to show this.

We need not here trace the historical process by which capitalist market societies developed out of earlier societies based on rank and status. Nor need we examine the logic by which a simple market society of independent producers, in which everyone had his own bit of land or capital to work on and simply exchanged his products in the market, would necessarily tend to develop into the full capitalist society, in which most people work on other people's capital. We need only notice that the characteristic and essential relationship between people in a fully-developed capitalist society is that most people have not got enough land or capital of their own to work on and consequently have to work on someone else's. I am not concerned here with any question of the justice of such an arrangement; a case can be made either way about that. I am simply concerned to point out that capitalism would not be capitalism if the already accumulated capital, and the effective power to accumulate it, were not in the hands of a relatively small number of persons. It is their decisions, and their power to set people to work in ways they decide, that make the wheels go round.

But, you may say, if they pay people what they are worth (as they must do in a fully competitive market for labour) how can there be any such net transfer as we have spoken of, any net transfer of part of the employees' powers to the owners of the capital? It depends on how you define the powers of a man.

If you take the powers of a man to be simply the strength and skill which he possesses, then when he sells the use of that strength and skill to another at its market price there is no net transfer of any of his powers to another. He is selling something he owns for what it is worth: he gets no less than he gives.

But if you take the powers of man to be not just the strength and skill he possesses, but his ability to use that strength and skill to produce something, the case is altogether different. For then his powers must include not only his *capacity* to labour (that is, his strength and skill) but also his *ability* to labour, his ability to use his strength and skill. I do not see how any narrower a definition of the powers of a man is consistent with his essential human quality. The power of a horse or a machine may be defined as the amount of work it can do whether it is set to work or not. But a human being, to be human, must be able to use his strength and skill for purposes he has consciously formed. So the powers of a man must include his being able to put his strength and skill to work. His powers must therefore include access to something to work on, access to the land or materials or other capital without which his capacity to labour cannot become active labour and so cannot produce anything or do anything to his purpose. A man's powers, in short, must include access to what I have called the means of labour.

If a man's powers must include access to the means of labour, then his powers are diminished when he has less than free access to the means of labour. If he has no access, his powers are reduced to zero and he ceases to live, unless he is rescued by some dispensation from outside the competitive market. If he can get some access but cannot get it for nothing, then his powers are reduced by the amount of them that he has to hand over to get the necessary access. This is exactly the situation most men are in, and necessarily so, in the capitalist market society. They must, in the nature of the system, permit a net transfer of part of their powers to those who own the means of labour.

It is in this sense that the relations between individuals in the capitalist society are power relations, relations involving the transfer of part of some men's powers to others. And it is for this reason that we can speak of the liberal state, whose job it is to maintain and enforce these relations, as a double system of power. If the liberal state is a double system of power, so too is the liberal-democratic state, for as we saw, the liberal-democratic state is essentially the liberal state with a democratic franchise added. That such a transfer is a necessary characteristic of any capitalist market society is commonly overlooked. It is obscured by the more obvious fact about capitalism, that it has been enormously more productive than any previous system, and so has been able to afford a higher material standard for everybody than could any previous system. Indeed, capitalism by its very nature produces more than could be produced by a society of peasants and craftsmen, each owning his own means of labour and exchanging merely his products. In such a society of individual independent producers, there would be no net transfer of individual powers, provided that the market for their products was fully competitive: no one would be getting more out of the others than the others were getting out of him. But nobody would be getting much. Compared with such a simple market society, the greater productivity of capitalism can, and generally does, more than offset the transfer of part of their powers from the working force, at least for all except the lowest one-quarter or so who are at or below the poverty line.

This being the case, why should we make such a point of there being this compulsive transfer in even the most freely competitive capitalist society? What is the use of an analytical exercise that resolves an existing system into two forces always moving in opposite directions, if each of the two forces must be accompanied by the other? We have seen that the transfer of powers is necessary to the high productivity of capitalism. So why not just look at the net result of the counteracting forces, instead of separating them out? If the higher productivity more than offsets the compulsive transfer, why not just look at the balance, and leave it at that?

The reason for not leaving it at that is quite simple. The reason is that it is now possible, as it was not possible in the heyday of capitalism, to conceive of a system in which high productivity does not require the transfer of powers from non-owners. Not only is it *possible* to conceive of such a system; it *has* been conceived, and is being attempted, in the socialist third of the world. Whether or not their alternative system can be made to work as it is intended to, we have to reckon with the fact that it is in full spate, and that it is attractive to the imagination of the newly-independent underdeveloped countries as well. It is one of history's meanest tricks that the enormous advances in productivity that were made by capitalism, and could not have been made in any other way, can now possibly be taken over by those who have rejected capitalism. But history is no respecter of the past.

We seem to have come a long way round in this lecture to make a single point about the nature of capitalist society, but the relevance of that point to the contemporary problems of liberal-democracy should now be apparent. Because liberal-democracy developed out of the liberal state and the capitalist society, it still leans heavily on the justifying theory of the capitalist market. But liberal-democracy has now to compete with other visions of society, which are more aware than we have generally been of the elementary forces at work in ours. We need to be more aware of them too, if we are to give ourselves a chance to compete.

The Myth of Maximization

5

The liberal-democratic state which we in the West now enjoy is, we have seen, a historical compound of the liberal state, which was not democratic at all to begin with, and the democratic franchise, which was added to it later. The liberal state was a matter of having competing political parties and having certain guaranteed freedoms—freedom of association, of speech and publication, of religion, and freedom of the person, that is, freedom from arbitrary arrest and imprisonment. These freedoms were seen to be both good in themselves and necessary to the working of a competitive party system. The job of the liberal state was, and was seen to be, to provide the conditions for a capitalist market society. The essence both of the liberal state and the market society was competition, competition between individuals who were free to choose what they would do with their own energies and skills, and free to choose whom they would authorize, as governments, to make and enforce the rules which were needed for the competitive market society. The liberal state was the politics of choice, in the service of a society of choices. It had no necessary connection with democracy; indeed, as we have seen, until well on in the nineteenth century the liberal state was generally thought to be endangered by democracy.

Yet when competition and freedom of choice are set up as general principles, when they are proclaimed to be a good thing, or even *the* good thing, logic demands that everybody be allowed into the competition. This is the point that was pressed by those who had had no vote in the original liberal state. Their view finally prevailed. Not that there is any natural affinity between politicians and logic, but that the politicians of the day became aware that if they did not yield to logic they might have to yield to force. By the time the liberal state was democratized, the old idea of democracy had been liberalized. We may even say that the countries which successfully made the transition from the non-democratic liberal state to the liberal-democratic state are those in which the old idea of democracy, as rule by and for the poor, had been converted to the idea of democracy as the right to get into the competition.

The notion of democracy has always contained the notion of equality. Not arithmetical equality of income or wealth, but equality of opportunity to realize one's human capacities. This is what had been denied in the pre-liberal societies, where many men had been slaves or serfs or at least had been held down to inferior positions which prevented them from realizing their potentialities as individuals. The goal of the liberal revolutions was to end this state of affairs and to open up opportunity to everyone. This goal provided some common ground on which those who wanted a competitive liberal society and those who wanted a more equal society could meet. This is probably the reason why the liberal revolutions could generally enlist some popular support.

Yet equality of opportunity can mean very different things. It can mean an equal right to a fully human life for all who will exert themselves: on this interpretation it comes to about the same thing as the classic democratic vision of an equal society. Or equality of opportunity can mean an equal legal right to get into the competitive race for more for oneself: on this interpretation it comes to about the same thing as the classic liberal vision of the market society. It was this second interpretation that came to prevail, and it has set the tone of our present liberal-democratic societies. Everyone can be in the race, indeed everyone has to be in the race. But, as we saw in the last lecture, everybody cannot be in it on equal terms. For in the nature of the

capitalist market society there must be some who own the capital
on which others must work. Those without enough capital on
which to work have to pay for access to others' capital. They
have to pay for access to what I have called the means of labour.
They have to submit to a net transfer of part of their powers to
other persons.

This transfer of powers, I have said, generally goes unnoticed
because it is overshadowed by the greater productivity of the
capitalist economy. It is when this productivity declines, as in the
great depression of the 1930s, that the transfer is really noticed.
And it is then seen to affect not only those whose sole resource is
their own labour but also those who have some little capital as
well. Independent family farmers then find they are no longer
independent if much of their working capital is borrowed.

It is then that both industrial workers and farmers are apt to
turn to radical political action, designed to reduce the transfer
of powers, or even to end it. Such action has sometimes succeeded
in reducing it, at least from the extreme it reaches in a depression, by getting the state to set up systems of transfer payments
in the other direction. Social insurance and other benefits of the
welfare state, to the extent that they are paid for by graduated
taxes on wealth and income, are a transfer in the other direction.

The welfare state has pretty clearly come to stay. It is the
norm in liberal-democratic capitalist societies now. But we must
notice that the offsetting transfers which the welfare state provides can never, within capitalism, equal the original and continuing transfer. This is fully appreciated by the strongest
defenders of capitalism, who point out, quite rightly, that if welfare transfers got so large as to eat up profits there would be no
more incentive to capitalist enterprise, and so no more capitalist
enterprise. As long as we enjoy the benefits of capitalism, then,
we must put up with the compulsive transfer of part of the
powers of non-owners to owners. We don't mind putting up with
this, indeed we don't even notice it, while capitalism is producing
the goods.

A great many thoughtful people, reflecting on the nature of
their society, may find this sketch of its anatomy unfamiliar and
unconvincing. Professional people who work for public or semi-
public bodies which are not in business for profit will not recog-

nize any net transfer of part of their powers to those who own the capital on which they work. Teachers and social workers, librarians and civil servants, are not obviously having part of their powers transferred to others who are owners of their means of labour. Must we then redraw the anatomy of our society to take account of the large number of such people in it? I think not. For the amount of reward such people get for their work is determined by the amount that people of comparable skill and length of training can get in the profit-making sector of the economy. This is so whether or not their skills are of a kind that can be marketed in the profit-making sector as well as in the non-profit sector of the society. Some professions afford little or no possibility of moving back and forth between the two sectors, but salaries cannot be higher in the non-profit sector than in the profit sector or everybody deciding on a career would go into the non-profit sector. So the rate of reward for comparable skills and lengths of training cannot, in a free market economy, be higher in the non-profit sector than in the profit sector. But the rate of reward in the profit sector is necessarily one which allows a transfer of part of the person's powers to the owners of the means of his labour. To whom, then, is the transfer made in the case of those working in the non-profit sector? It can only be to the public, to the whole local or regional or national community which has, through one agency or another, decided as a community to provide such services to itself.

The transfer of part of a man's powers to his own community does not seem to be a net transfer at all; for he seems to be getting it all back as a member of the community. But he isn't getting it all back: he is getting only part of it. Some of it is going to those members of the community who are contributing their powers not to the community but to private owners of the means of labour. So some part of his powers is being transferred away from him. This is unavoidable so long as we are using capitalist enterprise to look after the main productive work of the whole society.

We are confirmed, then, in our earlier conclusion that a capitalist market society necessarily involves a net transfer of part of the powers of some men to others. The politics of choice and the society of competition do contain, and generally conceal, a compulsive transfer of powers which is a diminution of the human essence. The fact that the transfer has only been severely felt in periods when the productive system has not been working very well, or in countries which are less prosperous than the most prosperous, does not alter the fact that the continuous transfer is built into the system.

Now all this did not matter very much as long as there were no alternative prospects or visions, no conceivable ways of reaching high productivity without this transfer of powers. But as we have seen, there are now alternative visions. The logic of capitalist society is in fact challenged. How satisfactory has our answer been?

An answer has been in the making for a long time now, for it is a long time ago—something like a century ago—that the most perceptive liberal thinkers saw that an answer was going to be needed. I think of that great liberal, John Stuart Mill, who saw, rather more than a century ago, that what he called the labouring classes would not put up with the existing transfer of powers much longer. He could not himself find a feasible answer. It was left to a subsequent generation of economists, in the 1870s and later, to provide something that has passed for an answer ever since. (It has to be said that most economists today are aware that it is not an answer, but it is still received as an answer in the general ideology of our liberal societies.)

The answer they provided really picked up from an earlier individualist theory which had been set out as early as the seventeenth century, when a new twist had been given to the traditional natural law idea. The traditional idea, which goes back as far as Aristotle, was that the human essence is activity in pursuit of a conscious, rational purpose. The new turn was to say that the essence of rational behaviour was maximization of individual satisfactions, or maximization of individual utilities. So the human essence was rational action which maximized utilities.

By the nineteenth century this Utilitarian theory had pretty well carried the day. It assumed that maximization of utilities was the ultimate good. It assumed that men's desires for all kinds of satisfactions are naturally unlimited, so that they will in fact go on seeking to maximize them. Since desires were unlimited, the means of satisfying them would always be scarce. The problem then was to find the system which would employ the scarce means to produce the maximum satisfactions. The problem was solved by demonstrating that the way to maximize utilities over the whole of a society was to leave everything to a competitive market economy, upheld by a liberal state. And the justifying theory of liberal-democracy has leaned heavily on this theory of maximization ever since.

The theory of maximization looked all right at first. Political economists could demonstrate that, taking as given everyone's resources of land and capital and labour, the maximum product would be got by leaving everyone to make the best bargain he could in a freely competitive market. Not only would this maximize the product, it would also distribute the whole product among all the individuals exactly in proportion to their contribution to it. This could be, and was, demonstrated with impeccable logic.

Yet although the justifying theory of liberal-democratic society still leans heavily on this theory of market maximization of utilities, it has become somewhat unsatisfactory as a justifying theory, for several reasons.

In the first place, it is only if incomes are taken as given that it is possible to demonstrate that the fully competitive market does maximize satisfactions. With any given distribution of resources and income you can show that the operation of the free market maximizes the returns to which everyone is entitled. But unless you can show that the existing distribution is fair you do not get a justification of the system.

Nor was it a sufficient way out of this to show, as could easily be shown, that in the fully competitive market everyone must get a reward exactly proportional to what he put in. For to make this an ethical justification of the system you would have to be able to show that the reward was proportional to the human energy and skill that each man put in. But this is just what could not be shown, because the rewards had to be proportional to *all* the factors of production, including the accumulated capital and natural resources that were contributed by the owners of them, and these could scarcely be shown to be owned in proportion to the human energy and skill expended by their owners.

So, even on the assumption of perfect competition, there was no adequate justification of the system. But on top of that, the natural development of the capitalist market has been away from the perfect competition that was assumed in the theory. The proof that the production of utilities would be maximized by the natural operation of the market requires the assumption of a market so fully competitive that no one person or combination of persons can control any prices. Only if every enterpriser had to take as given by the market, the prices for what he needed to buy and what he was considering producing for sale, only then would the system of enterprise produce what was wanted most efficiently. Only so would the scarce means at the disposal of the society be automatically directed by the market mechanism to the production of the desired goods and services. Only so, that is to say, would the market maximize utilities.

But the advanced capitalist economies have long since reached the stage at which large corporate enterprises, or groups of them, are able to control the output and prices of a good many things. To the extent that they are able to do so, their decisions about production are not determined by the market, and there is no reason to expect that their decisions will contribute to the maximizing of utilities over the whole society.

The virtue of the fully competitive market is that all the individuals and firms in it, who are all assumed to be trying to maximize their own profit or utility, can do so only by behaviour that maximizes utility over the whole society. What is constant in any market society is that everyone is trying to get the most he can. But it is only where there is perfect competition that this behaviour leads to maximization of utilities over the whole society. Where competition is removed, the firms go on maximizing their profits, but this no longer maximizes social utility.

But whether we go on assuming effective competition as the norm, or whether we make allowances for the decline of competition and the rise of price-making corporations, the theory that the market maximizes utilities is not much good as a justification of the market society. It is not much good because it begs the question. That is, if the theory is to be a justification as well as an explanation of the market economy, it has to take for granted what it is supposed to prove. It has to take for granted that a certain distribution of income is justifiable, and that the market distributes rewards in accordance with some justifiable pattern of human deserts.

We can I think neglect here certain further difficulties about the idea of maximization of utilities, but they may be mentioned in passing. How can you add together the satisfactions or utilities that different people get from different things? How can you compare them on a single measuring scale? There is, to say the least, no obvious way of doing so. But if you can't do so, then you can't say that one assortment of satisfactions is the maximum one. You can't say that one set of utilities available for the whole society, one set consisting of so many units of x and so many units of y and so on, adds up to a larger total of utility than some other set that might have been made available. The only way of avoiding this difficulty is to say that every society does make a rough and ready moral judgment of the relative human value of different goods, putting so many pyramids ahead of so many more homely delights, or so much milk for school children ahead of so many yachts.

But of course if you allow such a measuring scale you are not leaving things to the operation of the market, and you cannot then claim that the market does maximize the satisfaction of the spontaneous desires of all the separate individuals.

However, we need not spend any time on the logical difficulties of the theory that the market maximizes utilities over a whole society. We can neglect those difficulties because they are not the most serious ones when we are looking at the theory as a justification of the competitive market society. The serious difficulties, in this context, are the ones we noticed at the beginning. First, the market can only be shown to maximize utilities when a certain income distribution is taken as given: the market can only maximize the satisfactions people can afford to buy. And secondly, the market cannot reward people in proportion to the energy and skill they expend, since it has to reward ownership as well. It has to look after the transfer of powers that we spoke of earlier.

We have perhaps spent too long on this theory of maximization, which I think we are now entitled to call the myth of maximization. What has it got to do with the prospects of liberal-democracy, which is, after all, our central concern in these lectures? Quite a lot, I think. For our liberal-democracies seem to be relying more heavily on the myth of maximization the more they feel themselves challenged ideologically by the two-thirds of the world that has rejected the ethics of competition. It is time we realized that the theory of maximization isn't good enough in the kind of contest we are now in, and are bound to continue in for the foreseeable future.

I want to suggest that our moral and political theory took the wrong turning when it began to interpret the human essence as possession or acquisition. I said, earlier in this lecture, that before the rise of the all-inclusive market society the traditional view had been that the human essence was activity in pursuit of a conscious rational purpose. Then, with the rise of the market society, the essence of rational purpose was taken to be the pursuit of maximum material possessions. This was a fairly realistic conclusion at the time, because with the rise of the market society, possessions were becoming the only effective means an individual could have to the achievement of any rational purpose. The liberal theory of man and society, being developed to explain and justify the market society, had this emphasis on possessiveness embedded in it from the beginning.

Yet as a social theory it left a good deal to be desired. For as soon as you take the essence of man to be the acquisition of more *things* for himself, as soon as you make the essential human quality the striving for possessions rather than creative activity, you are caught up in an insoluble contradiction. Human beings are sufficiently unequal in strength and skill that if you put them into an unlimited contest for possessions, some will not only get more than others, but will get control of the means of labour to which the others must have access. The others then cannot be fully human even in the restricted sense of being able to get possessions, let alone in the original sense of being able to use their faculties in purposive creative activity. So in choosing to make the essence of man the striving for possessions, we make it impossible for many men to be fully human. By defining man as an infinite appropriator we make it impossible for many men to qualify as men.

You may say we have no choice. You may say that men do in fact have limitless desires, and will try to satisfy them by acquiring more possessions in every way they are allowed to do. So, as soon as we recognize that men are in fact unequal in strength and skill, we have no alternative but to put up with the fact that some will get more. You may say that we have to put up with it, even though it makes some men less human than others. If we leave men at all free in their human capacity as appropriators we must acquiesce in the denial of full humanity to a substantial part of mankind. If we refuse to permit this denial of humanity we have to set up another denial: we have to deny men the freedom to try to satisfy their naturally unlimited desires by the acquisition of property. And this also appears as a denial of humanity. There does not seem much hope of avoiding one contradiction or the other. Either way, to assert full humanity is to deny it. The record of past societies, those preceding the full market society, seems only to confirm the dilemma. For they generally denied freedom, and even so did not maintain equality.

But we may find some hope in the fact that the dilemma has always been an offshoot of scarcity, and that we are now, thanks to the technological advances made by capitalist enterprise, within sight of a society of abundance. The paradox, a very pleasant paradox, is that the idea of scarcity in relation to limitless desires was itself largely a creation of the market society, and that the advances in productivity made by the capitalist market system are now making the idea out of date.

We shall have to consider, in the final lecture, whether the prospect of a society of abundance, replacing an economy of scarcity, will allow our liberal-democratic market society to overcome the contradiction that has been inherent in it so far. The question is whether, and on what terms, we can move from a society that has necessarily diminished our humanity by defining it as possession, to a society which will reinstate humanity as creative activity.

The Near Future
of Democracy and
6 # Human Rights

In the first lecture of this series I raised certain questions about the future of democracy. And in the five lectures so far I have drawn attention to some facts about the present world position of democracy which are often neglected or under-rated, and have pointed to some of the implications of these facts. We might pause now to take stock, to see whether the results of our factual analysis so far can help us with our original questions or with any reformulation of the questions which might now seem to be in order.

The original questions themselves arose from the recognition of one new fact about democracy, or rather, from the conjunction of this new fact with an older-established one. The new fact was that the Western democracies no longer have or expect to have a monopoly of civilization or world leadership, but that two other concepts of democracy now share the world with us. These are the Soviet concept and the one that prevails in most of the newly-independent underdeveloped countries; both are embodied in actually operating political systems, and both are non-liberal.

This new fact impinges on the somewhat older fact that the great majority of people in the Western liberal-democracies place a high value on the unique characteristics of the liberal-democratic state. What is valued most highly is the civil liberties which it generally affords: freedom of speech, freedom of association, and freedom from arbitrary arrest and detention. Beyond that, we value the way our governments can be held somewhat responsible to the majority will through the competition of political parties, parties which can be freely formed and between which individuals are free to choose at the periodical general elections which authorize governments. These civil and political liberties, though far from perfectly realized in liberal-democracies, are their unique achievement, and we put a high value on them.

So there are two facts. The one is that we put a high value on these liberties. The other is that liberal-democracy now has to live in a world two-thirds of which is practising some other political system, and practising or aspiring to some other kind of society. It is the conjunction of these two facts that raises the important questions for democracy today. The questions I proposed arose directly or indirectly out of this new situation. Can we keep our unique system? Or can we keep what we most value in it?

These were our questions. What material have we for dealing with them? We might summarize the propositions that have come out of our analysis.

First, the liberal-democratic state was liberal and market-oriented first and democratic later. That is to say, the democratic franchise was a later addition to a well-established liberal state, the mechanism of which was competitive non-democratic parties, and the purpose of which was to provide the conditions for a competitive, capitalist, market society. By the time the liberal state was democratized, the demand of the democratic forces was to get into the competition, not to discard it for any other kind of social order.

Second, the democratic franchise was used to turn the old liberal *laissez-faire* state into a welfare and regulatory state. The change would have taken place anyway, since the politicians of the day were aware that this was necessary to buy off politically dangerous discontent. But the welfare and regulatory state has not altered the essential nature of the capitalist market society. The proof of this depends on our third proposition.

Third, the capitalist market society necessarily contains a continuous transfer of part of the powers of some men to others. It does so because it requires concentrated ownership and control, in relatively few hands, of the capital and resources which are the only means of labour for the rest. Since the rest must have access to the means of labour, they must pay for that access by a transfer of part of their powers (or part of the product of their powers) to the owners of the means of labour. The welfare state may enforce transfers in the other direction, but these can never be as large as the original and continuing transfer. For that would kill capitalist enterprise, whereas the welfare state relies on capitalist enterprise to carry on the main productive work of the society. The welfare state is only a variation on the theme of capitalist market society.

Fourth, on any non-slavish definition of the powers of a man, or of the human essence as the rational pursuit of conscious purposes, the transfer of part of the powers of a man that is inherent in the capitalist market society is a diminution of the human essence.

Fifth, while the justifying theory of the liberal-democratic market society has leaned heavily on the theory that the fully competitive market maximizes utilities over the whole society, the maximizing theory is demonstrably inadequate to justify the system, for it assumes what it is supposed to prove. You can only demonstrate that the market maximizes utilities if you take for granted a given distribution of incomes: the market only maximizes the satisfactions people can afford to buy. And in a capitalist market society, however fully competitive, incomes cannot be proportional to people's expenditure of energy and skill, because the market has to reward ownership as well as exertion. Moreover, we have moved a long way from the fully competitive market: to the extent that corporations can control output and prices, their decisions no longer contribute to the maximizing of utilities over the whole society.

Sixth, in the justifying theories of all three kinds of democracy the ultimate ethical principle, at the highest level of generality, is the same. In each case the aim is to provide the conditions for the free development of human capacities, and to do this equally for all members of the society. In each case the essence of man is taken to be activity in pursuit of a rational conscious purpose.

And in each case the realization of this essence is seen to require both freedom and equality: freedom of each individual from subservience to the wills of others, and equality in this freedom.

It is when we move down from the highest level of generality that the serious differences between the three kinds become apparent. It will be sufficient here, in summary, to concentrate on the distinction between the liberal and the non-liberal types, which we may try to state in the next two propositions.

Seventh, the non-liberal concepts of democracy, that is, the Marxian concept which prevails in the Soviet countries, and what we may call the Rousseauan concept which is more typical of the newly-independent underdeveloped countries, have one thing in common. They both hold that the requisite equality of human rights or human freedom cannot be provided in a market society, and therefore they put first on their agenda the move away from the market society. They are not interested in the freedom of individual acquisition of property, for they find this to be not only not necessary to but inconsistent with their vision of real human freedom and equal human rights. Nor do they give a high priority in their scale of values to the political freedoms. Believing as they do that the most important thing is the reformation of society, and realizing that this requires political power, they are not prepared to encourage or even allow such political freedoms as might hinder their power to reform the society. Thus political freedoms come a poor second to the drive for the new kind of society they believe to be necessary for the realization of equal human rights. Freedom is sacrificed to equality; or, more accurately, present freedoms are sacrificed to a vision of fuller and more equal freedom in the future. Freedom, in this view, contradicts itself: to get it in the future is to deny it in the present.

Eighth, the liberal concept of democracy, emphasizing the present freedoms of the market society and the political freedoms of a competitive party system, is caught up in a different contradiction. The freedom of the market society necessarily includes the freedom to acquire material possessions. Freedom of acquisition is absolutely essential, for the market society relies on the motive of acquisition to get the work of the society done. Freedom of acquisition is so necessary to the market society that it tends to take first place in the scale of values. But this freedom contradicts itself. For given the natural inequalities of strength and skill, freedom of acquisition leads to some men getting possession of the capital and resources that are the means of labour for all the others. This makes it impossible for the others to have freedom of acquisition: they have to pay for access to the means of labour with the loss of some of their powers.

Ninth, the technological advances made by capitalism have enormously increased our material productivity, with different effects on freedom and the human essence in different parts of the world. In the West, the sheer increase in the volume of material satisfactions has overshadowed the shortcomings of capitalist society in respect of freedom and of equality of individual opportunity to realize the human essence. At the same time, in the non-capitalist countries, the need for increasing productivity is largely responsible for their greater lack of freedom. The effort to catch up with the high productivity of capitalism, starting from a low base, requires a compulsive accumulation of social capital by the use of state power. It requires, that is to say, more, and more obvious, compulsions than are required in an advanced capitalist society with an already accumulated stock of capital.

Tenth, we have to expect, as a result of automation and the discovery and control of new sources of non-human energy, increases in productivity in the next few decades far exceeding the increases of the past, both in amount and in speed. But since these increases can now be expected not only in the most advanced capitalist countries but also in the most advanced socialist countries, the increases will not be attributable to capitalism and so will not automatically be taken to offset the shortcomings of capitalist society. On the contrary, such future increases in productivity will heighten two effects that are already apparent as a result of recent increases. First, the liberal, capitalist ethos will have to meet increasingly stiff ideological competition from the Soviet, socialist ethos. And second, the level of expectation of the underdeveloped peoples will increase, thus increasing their present sense of injustice at the unequal distribution of human opportunity between the rich countries (which are mostly capitalist) and the poor countries. This sense of injustice is already pressing somewhat on the conscience of the West, and the moral feedback is likely to get stronger.

With these ten propositions before us we may return to our central question. Can we in the liberal-democracies retain the values of freedom and individuality that we most cherish?

I shall suggest that the communist revolutions, and the revolutions in the underdeveloped countries, which together seem to threaten our way of life, may be the saving of it. If we read the lessons of these revolutions properly, they may lead us to a recognition of what we have to do to retain and strengthen our liberal values. Liberal values have now to compete, as they never had to do before, with non-liberal democratic values. But the very thing that has brought competitors to the liberal society into the field can release us from the dilemma which has plagued the liberal capitalist society up to now. What has brought competitors into the field is the fact, and the prospect, that the present and future productive techniques of capitalism can be transferred to non-capitalist societies, and can in those societies be used to enlarge the freedom and humanity of man. This same prospective increase in productive powers can, if we will it and if we see what we are about, release us from the dilemma of the liberal capitalist market society. For the dilemma exists only when it is assumed, as the Western market societies have up to now assumed, that the permanent condition of mankind is a condition of scarcity in relation to unlimited desires. The dilemma has been that if we allow freedom to naturally unequal individuals, we are in fact denying equal freedom and humanity to all but the stronger and more skilful. For to allow freedom of enterprise and of acquisition has been to deny equal access to the means of labour, that is, to deny equal access to the means of a fully human life. The choice had to be made between freedom along with denial of full humanity to all but the stronger and more skilful, or denial of freedom in the interest of more equal chances of humanity. The liberal capitalist society chose freedom and denial of full humanity. The choice no longer has to be made. It had to be made only while scarcity was king, and while, therefore, the incentive of unlimited freedom of acquisition was needed to get the increased production that was desired.

The implacable force in the drama of liberal society was scarcity in relation to unlimited desire. It was scarcity and unlimited desire that made the drama, and while it lasted it was tragedy. But now we can see it for what it has become, melodrama. Scarcity in relation to unlimited desire can now be seen for what it is, merely the villain in a melodrama, who can be disposed of before the play is finished. We can begin to recognize now that the vision of scarcity in relation to unlimited desire was a creation of the capitalist market society. Certainly, before the advent of that society, nobody assumed that unlimited desire was the natural and proper attribute of the human being. You do not find it in Aristotle or in St. Thomas Aquinas. You begin to find it only with the rise of the capitalist market society in the seventeenth century, in Hobbes and in Locke, and it is carried to its logical conclusion by James Mill, at the beginning of the nineteenth century, for whom the "grand governing law of human nature" was the insatiable desire of every man for power to render the person and properties of others subservient to his pleasures.

The dilemma was still a real one when James Mill grappled with it. But it is no longer so. We have been, or rather we can be, liberated from the dilemma of scarcity by the new productivity of which we dispose in prospect. We can see now that men are not by nature infinitely desirous creatures, but were only made so by the market society, which compelled men to seek ever greater power in order to maintain even a modest level of satisfactions.

It may seem odd to say that scarcity was invented with the market society, and by market men. Had not mankind always lived in penury, at least ever since some supposed golden age back in the mists of time? Yet in a very real sense scarcity was an invention of market society. What was invented was the notion of scarcity as a thing to be overcome. Scarcity was set up as the condition whose conquest was to be the great object of human endeavour. Scarcity was thus put in the forefront of human consciousness. But it was only put there when the emerging capitalist market society needed it as an organizing principle. The concept of scarcity became central and dominant only as capitalist society set about overcoming it. Scarcity was created by the very process of organizing to overcome it. An overmastering consciousness of scarcity had to be created in order to justify the capitalist society and to give it its driving force. An all-pervasive awareness of scarcity was needed both to justify the operations of those who came out at the top and to motivate those who stayed below and had to be made to work harder than they had worked before.

We don't need this dominant concept of scarcity any longer. We don't need any longer the morality which gives pride of place to the motive of acquisition. We don't need any longer the incentive of unlimited freedom of acquisition. In at least the most advanced capitalist countries, we produce already more commodities and more new capital than we know what to do with. And in the very near future our problem will be not to get people to work but to find something for them to do, not to make the most efficient use of scarce means but to start repairing the scarcity of the human values that have been submerged in the struggle against material scarcity.

How great a change is possible and is required was foreseen thirty-five years ago by the most eminent English liberal of our century, the great economist John Maynard Keynes. In an essay entitled "Economic Possibilities for Our Grandchildren" and dated 1930, he wrote this:

> When the accumulation of wealth is no longer of high social importance, there will be great changes in the code of morals. We shall be able to rid ourselves of many of the pseudo-moral principles which have hag-ridden us for two hundred years, by which we have exalted some of the most distasteful of human qualities into the position of the highest virtues. We shall be able to afford to dare to assess the money-motive at its true value.... All kinds of social customs and economic practices, affecting the distribution of wealth and of economic rewards and penalties, which we now maintain at all costs, however distasteful and unjust they may be in themselves, because they are tremendously useful in promoting the accumulation of capital, we shall then be free, at last, to discard.
>
> ... We shall once more value ends above means and prefer the good to the useful.
>
> ... But [he added] beware! The time for all this is not yet. For at least another hundred years we must pretend to ourselves and to everyone that fair is foul and foul is fair; for foul is useful and fair is not. Avarice and usury and precaution must be our gods for a little longer still. For only they can lead us out of the tunnel of economic necessity into daylight.*

Keynes gave it a hundred years from 1930. But the pace of change has quickened so much since he wrote, that we may judge the time to discard the morality of scarcity has already arrived.

*J. M. Keynes: *Essays in Persuasion* (London, 1932) pp. 369-72.

By discarding it, and only by discarding it, we can resolve the contradiction implicit in the market concept of freedom and in the market concept of the human essence, which concepts, we saw, were built into the liberal-democratic justifying theory. We can then hope to retrieve the democratic values of equal freedom and equal access to a rational purposive life.

This is all very well, you may say, but how can we expect to do it? There are indeed two large objections to be overcome. The first is an objection about power. Individuals and nations in the liberal-democratic world, after centuries of operating their competitive market societies, are so accustomed to acquisitive behaviour and seeking power over others that they cannot easily be got out of this frame of mind. It may be economically possible now for them to drop it; it may be desirable that they should drop it; but how can they drop it when the whole structure of their society has come to depend on power-seeking, both individual and national, both economic and political?

The second objection that must be met is an objection about the conquest of scarcity. There has been, you may say, one enormous oversight in my account of the imminent conquest of material scarcity: it has overlooked the fact that there is, and will be for a long time yet, tremendous poverty, tremendous material scarcity, in the underdeveloped countries. And in somewhat lesser degree the same is true of all but the most advanced of the communist countries. Perhaps then Lord Keynes's estimate of a hundred years before we could discard the morality of scarcity was not too long after all.

I do not think this objection can be sustained, and when we see why not we shall see an answer to the first objection also. This second objection cannot be sustained because the underdeveloped countries and the communist countries have undertaken the conquest of material scarcity by methods other than the acquisitive, individual power-seeking, methods of the market societies. They rejected the market morality from the beginning. They are trying to conquer scarcity without relying on the morality of scarcity.

Moreover (and this brings us towards an answer to the first objection), the communist countries who have been at it longer than the newly-independent underdeveloped countries, have already shown that they can do without the acquisitive market morality and still be very powerful. Even the underdeveloped countries, while not militarily or economically powerful compared with either the capitalist or communist great powers, have succeeded in getting a voice in world affairs which can scarcely now be taken from them and which is likely to increase. To that extent, even they now have some power.

I emphasize the power that the communist and the underdeveloped countries have attained because I think it is crucial in one respect not usually noticed. They have shown that power does not necessarily depend on market motivation and market morality. They have rejected the market and have not lost but gained strength. Market behaviour is no longer the sole source of power.

When the implications of this fact are realized they go far to meet the first of our two objections. The objection was that individuals and nations in the West cannot be expected to drop their acquisitive behaviour and their morality of scarcity because these are the way to power, and they are too thoroughly impregnated with the desire for power to be able to renounce the behaviour and morality that have given them power.

This difficulty disappears when it is seen that acquisitive market behaviour is no longer the sole source of power. Individuals and nations will no doubt go on seeking to increase their powers, but they need no longer do so by putting material acquisitiveness ahead of more equal freedoms. Indeed, not only need they not seek an increase of their power in this way, they are unlikely to get it this way.

We are in for a long contest for power and influence between West and East (with the underdeveloped countries being an increasingly significant factor). Warfare between great powers is no longer a possible way of settling the balance of power; the development of nuclear weapons has made that abundantly clear. Hence the relative power and influence of different nations and sections of the world is going to have to depend on the degree to which their economic and political systems satisfy the desires of all their people. Insofar as all these nations are democratic (in any one of the three ways we have seen), the desires of their people can be expected to be for equal access to the means of a decent life, or equal human rights.

The societies that have rejected the capitalist system will have both a moral advantage and a moral disadvantage in meeting that desire. The moral advantage is that they do not diminish any man's satisfaction by a compulsive transfer of part of his powers to others for the benefit of others. The moral disadvantage is that they do not provide the same measure of political freedoms and civil liberties, which are also essential human rights, as do the liberal capitalist countries.

Now there is no way of calculating generally the relative weight that any people will give to these moral advantages and disadvantages. We cannot come up with a plus or minus rating that would be universally agreed on for any actual society, and therefore we cannot establish a certainly valid balance of moral advantage as between two societies. But if we can predict *changes* in the weight or amount of any of the factors in either or both of the societies, and if the predicted changes are not the same in the different kinds of society, we can speak of probable changes in the net moral advantage of one kind of society as compared with the other. I think we can predict that the non-capitalist countries will retain the moral advantage they now enjoy in not having a compulsive transfer of powers, and that they will decrease their moral disadvantage about political and civil liberties. They have every reason to introduce political and civil liberties as soon as they can afford them, for a police state is a costly and treacherous thing for any set of rulers. And they are more able to afford them the more successful they are in reaching a high level of productivity which enables the other real wants of the people to be met, and so affords a natural basis for a stable political system.

Now if the liberal capitalist countries merely retain their present moral advantage and disadvantage, the net balance of advantage will tip against them, and they will decline in relative power. The societies which can best meet the demand of their own people for equal human rights, equal freedom for their members to realize their essential humanity, will be the ones that survive. What I am suggesting is that in the world from now on, power and influence will depend on moral advantage. And I am suggesting that we in the West will decline in power unless we can discard our possessive market morality. Power-oriented as we are, this argument should surely be decisive.

Moralists and theologians have been saying for a long time that we have got our values all wrong, in putting acquisition ahead of spiritual values. This has not cut much ice in the last three or four centuries because it was inconsistent with the search for individual and national power to which market societies have been committed. But if I am right in saying that national power from now on is going to depend on moral advantage, on moral stature, then the claims of morality and power will coincide. The way to national power will be the recognition and promotion of equal human rights. And the pursuit of these ends will bring an enlargement of individual power as well, not the powers of individuals over others or at the expense of others, but their powers to realize and enjoy their fullest human capacities.

I am very conscious that in these lectures I have raised more questions than I have answered, and that such answers as I have seen and suggested have not included specific recommendations for action. If you want an operative conclusion, it is this: tell your politicians that the free way of life depends, to an extent they have not yet dreamed of, on the Western nations remedying the inequality of human rights as between ourselves and the poor nations. Nothing less than massive aid, which will enable the poor nations to lift themselves to recognizable human equality, will now conserve the moral stature and the power of the liberal-democracies.